FORTY WEEKS

Daily Spiritual Record Book

William M. Watson, SJ

Other Books by William M. Watson, SJ

Sacred Story:
An Ignatian Examen for the Third Millennium

Inviting God into Your Life:
A Practical Guide for Prayer

Reflections and Homilies:
The Gonzaga Collection

Sacred Story Rosary:
An Ignatian Way to Pray the Mysteries

Sacred Story Affirmations

The Whole-Life Confession

My Sacred Story Missal

Understanding the Spiritual World

ACKNOWLEDGMENTS

To the dozens of people who asked Sacred Story
Institute for a daily spiritual record book
to help them remain faithful the
Sacred Story disciplines of FORTY WEEKS:

HERE YOU GO!

Sacred Story Press
1401 E Jefferson St, STE 405
Seattle, WA 98122

Copyright © 2018

Dedicated to Our Lady of the Way

Cover And Interior Art: Heart as a Path by Jerry Fenter
Jacket and Book Design: William Watson, SJ

Manufactured in the United States of America

ISBN-13: 978-1986393645
ISBN-10: 198639364X

INTRODUCTION

St. Ignatius used what he called a "marking system" and a spiritual journal to keep track of spiritual movements for his practice of the Examen. It is a helpful discipline that enabled him to "measure" both spiritual growth and the movements of consolation and desolation in his spiritual life.

This Spiritual Record Book is to be used to keep track of the spiritual disciplines associated with Sacred Story Prayer in *Forty Weeks*. The first fifteen weeks you are simply keeping track of the offering of your day and night to the Lord and something that both increased and decreased your "faith, hope and love" (if you can recall something from the day). This second practice is the important beginning of spiritual attention to your interior life.

When you begin Part Two and start the practice of the Sacred Story prayer version of the Examen, you are adding spiritual disciplines to your day. You have the option now of noting what you complete or don't compete each day.

You should not feel discouraged if you don't complete all the disciplines in a single day. Instead, use a review process to see what you are and are not doing. This can help you find a way to monitor how to be more faithful to the spiritual disciplines which are all geared to help you awaken to your own sacred story and your interior spiritual world.

Writing daily in the Spiritual Record Book also can help you keep faithful to the spiritual disciplines. Practice makes perfect!

Fr. Bill Watson, S.J.

 # Week I

SPIRITUAL RECORD

For Weeks 1-16, try to spend twenty minutes in the morning and in the evening without technology. When you awake, attune to the day,, and offer you day to God with a morning offering. When you go to sleep at night, have a space of tech-free time before you get into bed so you can hear your heart.

1. Prayer Upon Waking—*I attuned to the day ahead and invited God's help*

Location_____ *I did this*___(___Minutes) No___

2. As I Lie Down to Sleep—*I offered my heart and dreams to God*

Location_____ *I did this*___(___Minutes) No___

Desolation From the Day – <u>Write no more than two sentences</u> on what decreased *your faith, your hope, and your love for God and neighbor today.*

Consolation From the Day – <u>Write no more than two sentences</u> on what increased *your faith, your hope, and your love for God and neighbor today.*

SPIRITUAL RECORD

For Weeks 1-16, try to spend twenty minutes in the morning and in the evening without technology. When you awake, attune to the day, and offer you day to God with a morning offering. When you go to sleep at night, have a space of tech-free time before you get into bed so you can hear your heart.

1. Prayer Upon Waking—*I attuned to the day ahead and invited God's help*

Location_____   *I did this*___(___Minutes) No___

2. As I Lie Down to Sleep—*I offered my heart and dreams to God*

Location_____   *I did this*___(___Minutes) No___

Desolation From the Day – <u>Write no more than two sentences</u> on what decreased *your faith, your hope, and your love for God and neighbor today.*

Consolation From the Day – <u>Write no more than two sentences</u> on what increased *your faith, your hope, and your love for God and neighbor today.*

SPIRITUAL RECORD

For Weeks 1-16, try to spend twenty minutes in the morning and in the evening without technology. When you awake, attune to the day, and offer you day to God with a morning offering. When you go to sleep at night, have a space of tech-free time before you get into bed so you can hear your heart.

1. Prayer Upon Waking—*I attuned to the day ahead and invited God's help*

Location_____   *I did this*___(___Minutes) No___

2. As I Lie Down to Sleep—*I offered my heart and dreams to God*

Location_____   *I did this*___(___Minutes) No___

Desolation From the Day – <u>Write no more than two sentences</u> on what decreased *your faith, your hope, and your love for God and neighbor today.*

Consolation From the Day – <u>Write no more than two sentences</u> on what increased *your faith, your hope, and your love for God and neighbor today.*

SPIRITUAL RECORD

For Weeks 1-16, try to spend twenty minutes in the morning and in the evening without technology. When you awake, attune to the day, and offer you day to God with a morning offering. When you go to sleep at night, have a space of tech-free time before you get into bed so you can hear your heart.

1. Prayer Upon Waking—*I attuned to the day ahead and invited God's help*

Location_____   *I did this*___(___Minutes) No___

2. As I Lie Down to Sleep—*I offered my heart and dreams to God*

Location_____   *I did this*___(___Minutes) No___

Desolation From the Day – <u>Write no more than two sentences</u> on what decreased *your faith, your hope, and your love for God and neighbor today.*

Consolation From the Day – <u>Write no more than two sentences</u> on what increased *your faith, your hope, and your love for God and neighbor today.*

SPIRITUAL RECORD

For Weeks 1-16, try to spend twenty minutes in the morning and in the evening without technology. When you awake, attune to the day, and offer you day to God with a morning offering. When you go to sleep at night, have a space of tech-free time before you get into bed so you can hear your heart.

1. Prayer Upon Waking—*I attuned to the day ahead and invited God's help*

Location_____ *I did this*___(___Minutes) No___

2. As I Lie Down to Sleep—*I offered my heart and dreams to God*

Location_____ *I did this*___(___Minutes) No___

Desolation From the Day – <u>Write no more than two sentences</u> on what decreased *your faith, your hope, and your love for God and neighbor today.*

Consolation From the Day – <u>Write no more than two sentences</u> on what increased *your faith, your hope, and your love for God and neighbor today.*

SPIRITUAL RECORD

For Weeks 1-16, try to spend twenty minutes in the morning and in the evening without technology. When you awake, attune to the day, and offer you day to God with a morning offering. When you go to sleep at night, have a space of tech-free time before you get into bed so you can hear your heart.

1. Prayer Upon Waking—_I attuned to the day ahead and invited God's help_

Location_____ _I did this___(___Minutes)_ No___

2. As I Lie Down to Sleep—_I offered my heart and dreams to God_

Location_____ _I did this___(___Minutes)_ No___

Desolation From the Day – <u>Write no more than two sentences</u> **on what decreased** _your faith, your hope, and your love for God and neighbor today._

Consolation From the Day – <u>Write no more than two sentences</u> **on what increased** _your faith, your hope, and your love for God and neighbor today._

SPIRITUAL RECORD

For Weeks 1-16, try to spend twenty minutes in the morning and in the evening without technology. When you awake, attune to the day, and offer you day to God with a morning offering. When you go to sleep at night, have a space of tech-free time before you get into bed so you can hear your heart.

1. Prayer Upon Waking—*I attuned to the day ahead and invited God's help*

Location_____   *I did this*___(___Minutes) No___

2. As I Lie Down to Sleep—*I offered my heart and dreams to God*

Location_____   *I did this*___(___Minutes) No___

Desolation From the Day – <u>Write no more than two sentences</u> on what decreased *your faith, your hope, and your love for God and neighbor today.*

Consolation From the Day – <u>Write no more than two sentences</u> on what increased *your faith, your hope, and your love for God and neighbor today.*

Week 2

For Weeks 1-16, try to spend twenty minutes in the morning and in the evening without technology. When you awake, attune to the day, and offer you day to God with a morning offering. When you go to sleep at night, have a space of tech-free time before you get into bed so you can hear your heart.

1. Prayer Upon Waking—*I attuned to the day ahead and invited God's help*

Location_____ *I did this___(___Minutes) No___*

2. As I Lie Down to Sleep—*I offered my heart and dreams to God*

Location_____ *I did this___(___Minutes) No___*

Desolation From the Day – <u>Write no more than two sentences</u> on what decreased *your faith, your hope, and your love for God and neighbor today.*

Consolation From the Day – <u>Write no more than two sentences</u> on what increased *your faith, your hope, and your love for God and neighbor today.*

SPIRITUAL RECORD

For Weeks 1-16, try to spend twenty minutes in the morning and in the evening without technology. When you awake, attune to the day, and offer you day to God with a morning offering. When you go to sleep at night, have a space of tech-free time before you get into bed so you can hear your heart.

1. Prayer Upon Waking—*I attuned to the day ahead and invited God's help*

Location_____ *I did this*___(___Minutes) No___

2. As I Lie Down to Sleep—*I offered my heart and dreams to God*

Location_____ *I did this*___(___Minutes) No___

Desolation From the Day – <u>Write no more than two sentences</u> **on what decreased** *your faith, your hope, and your love for God and neighbor today.*

Consolation From the Day – <u>Write no more than two sentences</u> **on what increased** *your faith, your hope, and your love for God and neighbor today.*

SPIRITUAL RECORD

For Weeks 1-16, try to spend twenty minutes in the morning and in the evening without technology. When you awake, attune to the day, and offer you day to God with a morning offering. When you go to sleep at night, have a space of tech-free time before you get into bed so you can hear your heart.

1. Prayer Upon Waking—*I attuned to the day ahead and invited God's help*

Location_____ *I did this___(___Minutes) No___*

2. As I Lie Down to Sleep—*I offered my heart and dreams to God*

Location_____ *I did this___(___Minutes) No___*

Desolation From the Day – Write no more than two sentences **on what decreased** *your faith, your hope, and your love for God and neighbor today.*

Consolation From the Day – Write no more than two sentences **on what increased** *your faith, your hope, and your love for God and neighbor today.*

SPIRITUAL RECORD

For Weeks 1-16, try to spend twenty minutes in the morning and in the evening without technology. When you awake, attune to the day, and offer you day to God with a morning offering. When you go to sleep at night, have a space of tech-free time before you get into bed so you can hear your heart.

1. Prayer Upon Waking—*I attuned to the day ahead and invited God's help*

Location_____   *I did this*___(___Minutes) No___

2. As I Lie Down to Sleep—*I offered my heart and dreams to God*

Location_____   *I did this*___(___Minutes) No___

Desolation From the Day – <u>Write no more than two sentences</u> on what decreased *your faith, your hope, and your love for God and neighbor today.*

Consolation From the Day – <u>Write no more than two sentences</u> on what increased *your faith, your hope, and your love for God and neighbor today.*

SPIRITUAL RECORD

For Weeks 1-16, try to spend twenty minutes in the morning and in the evening without technology. When you awake, attune to the day, and offer you day to God with a morning offering. When you go to sleep at night, have a space of tech-free time before you get into bed so you can hear your heart.

1. Prayer Upon Waking—*I attuned to the day ahead and invited God's help*

Location_____   *I did this*___(___Minutes) No___

2. As I Lie Down to Sleep—*I offered my heart and dreams to God*

Location_____   *I did this*___(___Minutes) No___

Desolation From the Day – <u>Write no more than two sentences</u> on what decreased *your faith, your hope, and your love for God and neighbor today.*

Consolation From the Day – <u>Write no more than two sentences</u> on what increased *your faith, your hope, and your love for God and neighbor today.*

SPIRITUAL RECORD

For Weeks 1-16, try to spend twenty minutes in the morning and in the evening without technology. When you awake, attune to the day, and offer you day to God with a morning offering. When you go to sleep at night, have a space of tech-free time before you get into bed so you can hear your heart.

1. Prayer Upon Waking—*I attuned to the day ahead and invited God's help*

Location_____   *I did this*___(___Minutes) No___

2. As I Lie Down to Sleep—*I offered my heart and dreams to God*

Location_____   *I did this*___(___Minutes) No___

Desolation From the Day – <u>Write no more than two sentences</u> on what decreased *your faith, your hope, and your love for God and neighbor today.*

Consolation From the Day – <u>Write no more than two sentences</u> on what increased *your faith, your hope, and your love for God and neighbor today.*

SPIRITUAL RECORD

For Weeks 1-16, try to spend twenty minutes in the morning and in the evening without technology. When you awake, attune to the day, and offer you day to God with a morning offering. When you go to sleep at night, have a space of tech-free time before you get into bed so you can hear your heart.

1. Prayer Upon Waking—*I attuned to the day ahead and invited God's help*

Location_____ *I did this*___(___Minutes) No___

2. As I Lie Down to Sleep—*I offered my heart and dreams to God*

Location_____ *I did this*___(___Minutes) No___

Desolation From the Day – <u>Write no more than two sentences</u> on what decreased *your faith, your hope, and your love for God and neighbor today.*

Consolation From the Day – <u>Write no more than two sentences</u> on what increased *your faith, your hope, and your love for God and neighbor today.*

Week 3

For Weeks 1-16, try to spend twenty minutes in the morning and in the evening without technology. When you awake, attune to the day, and offer you day to God with a morning offering. When you go to sleep at night, have a space of tech-free time before you get into bed so you can hear your heart.

1. Prayer Upon Waking—*I attuned to the day ahead and invited God's help*

Location_____   *I did this___(___Minutes)* No___

2. As I Lie Down to Sleep—*I offered my heart and dreams to God*

Location_____   *I did this___(___Minutes)* No___

Desolation From the Day – <u>Write no more than two sentences</u> on what decreased *your faith, your hope, and your love for God and neighbor today.*

Consolation From the Day – <u>Write no more than two sentences</u> on what increased *your faith, your hope, and your love for God and neighbor today.*

SPIRITUAL RECORD

For Weeks 1-16, try to spend twenty minutes in the morning and in the evening without technology. When you awake, attune to the day, and offer you day to God with a morning offering. When you go to sleep at night, have a space of tech-free time before you get into bed so you can hear your heart.

1. Prayer Upon Waking—*I attuned to the day ahead and invited God's help*

Location_____ *I did this*___(___Minutes) No___

2. As I Lie Down to Sleep—*I offered my heart and dreams to God*

Location_____ *I did this*___(___Minutes) No___

Desolation From the Day – <u>Write no more than two sentences</u> on what decreased *your faith, your hope, and your love for God and neighbor today.*

Consolation From the Day – <u>Write no more than two sentences</u> on what increased *your faith, your hope, and your love for God and neighbor today.*

SPIRITUAL RECORD

For Weeks 1-16, try to spend twenty minutes in the morning and in the evening without technology. When you awake, attune to the day, and offer you day to God with a morning offering. When you go to sleep at night, have a space of tech-free time before you get into bed so you can hear your heart.

1. Prayer Upon Waking—*I attuned to the day ahead and invited God's help*

Location_____   *I did this*___(___Minutes) No___

2. As I Lie Down to Sleep—*I offered my heart and dreams to God*

Location_____   *I did this*___(___Minutes) No___

Desolation From the Day – <u>Write no more than two sentences</u> on what decreased *your faith, your hope, and your love for God and neighbor today.*

Consolation From the Day – <u>Write no more than two sentences</u> on what increased *your faith, your hope, and your love for God and neighbor today.*

SPIRITUAL RECORD

For Weeks 1-16, try to spend twenty minutes in the morning and in the evening without technology. When you awake, attune to the day, and offer you day to God with a morning offering. When you go to sleep at night, have a space of tech-free time before you get into bed so you can hear your heart.

1. Prayer Upon Waking—*I attuned to the day ahead and invited God's help*

Location_____ *I did this*___(___Minutes) No___

2. As I Lie Down to Sleep—*I offered my heart and dreams to God*

Location_____ *I did this*___(___Minutes) No___

Desolation From the Day – <u>Write no more than two sentences</u> on what decreased *your faith, your hope, and your love for God and neighbor today.*

Consolation From the Day – <u>Write no more than two sentences</u> on what increased *your faith, your hope, and your love for God and neighbor today.*

SPIRITUAL RECORD

For Weeks 1-16, try to spend twenty minutes in the morning and in the evening without technology. When you awake, attune to the day, and offer you day to God with a morning offering. When you go to sleep at night, have a space of tech-free time before you get into bed so you can hear your heart.

1. Prayer Upon Waking—*I attuned to the day ahead and invited God's help*

Location_____   *I did this*___(___Minutes) No___

2. As I Lie Down to Sleep—*I offered my heart and dreams to God*

Location_____   *I did this*___(___Minutes) No___

Desolation From the Day – <u>Write no more than two sentences</u> on what decreased *your faith, your hope, and your love for God and neighbor today.*

Consolation From the Day – <u>Write no more than two sentences</u> on what increased *your faith, your hope, and your love for God and neighbor today.*

SPIRITUAL RECORD

For Weeks 1-16, try to spend twenty minutes in the morning and in the evening without technology. When you awake, attune to the day, and offer you day to God with a morning offering. When you go to sleep at night, have a space of tech-free time before you get into bed so you can hear your heart.

1. Prayer Upon Waking—*I attuned to the day ahead and invited God's help*

Location_____   *I did this*___(___Minutes) No___

2. As I Lie Down to Sleep—*I offered my heart and dreams to God*

Location_____   *I did this*___(___Minutes) No___

Desolation From the Day – <u>Write no more than two sentences</u> on what decreased *your faith, your hope, and your love for God and neighbor today.*

Consolation From the Day – <u>Write no more than two sentences</u> on what increased *your faith, your hope, and your love for God and neighbor today.*

SPIRITUAL RECORD

For Weeks 1-16, try to spend twenty minutes in the morning and in the evening without technology. When you awake, attune to the day, and offer you day to God with a morning offering. When you go to sleep at night, have a space of tech-free time before you get into bed so you can hear your heart.

1. Prayer Upon Waking—*I attuned to the day ahead and invited God's help*

Location_____   *I did this*___(___Minutes) No___

2. As I Lie Down to Sleep—*I offered my heart and dreams to God*

Location_____   *I did this*___(___Minutes) No___

Desolation From the Day – <u>Write no more than two sentences</u> **on what decreased** *your faith, your hope, and your love for God and neighbor today.*

Consolation From the Day – <u>Write no more than two sentences</u> **on what increased** *your faith, your hope, and your love for God and neighbor today.*

Week 4

For Weeks 1-16, try to spend twenty minutes in the morning and in the evening without technology. When you awake, attune to the day, and offer you day to God with a morning offering. When you go to sleep at night, have a space of tech-free time before you get into bed so you can hear your heart.

1. Prayer Upon Waking—*I attuned to the day ahead and invited God's help*

Location_____   *I did this*____(____Minutes) No____

2. As I Lie Down to Sleep—*I offered my heart and dreams to God*

Location_____   *I did this*____(____Minutes) No____

Desolation From the Day – <u>Write no more than two sentences</u> on what decreased *your faith, your hope, and your love for God and neighbor today.*

Consolation From the Day – <u>Write no more than two sentences</u> on what increased *your faith, your hope, and your love for God and neighbor today.*

SPIRITUAL RECORD

For Weeks 1-16, try to spend twenty minutes in the morning and in the evening without technology. When you awake, attune to the day, and offer you day to God with a morning offering. When you go to sleep at night, have a space of tech-free time before you get into bed so you can hear your heart.

1. Prayer Upon Waking—*I attuned to the day ahead and invited God's help*

Location_____ *I did this____(____Minutes)* No____

2. As I Lie Down to Sleep—*I offered my heart and dreams to God*

Location_____ *I did this____(____Minutes)* No____

Desolation From the Day – <u>Write no more than two sentences</u> on what decreased *your faith, your hope, and your love for God and neighbor today.*

Consolation From the Day – <u>Write no more than two sentences</u> on what increased *your faith, your hope, and your love for God and neighbor today.*

SPIRITUAL RECORD

For Weeks 1-16, try to spend twenty minutes in the morning and in the evening without technology. When you awake, attune to the day, and offer you day to God with a morning offering. When you go to sleep at night, have a space of tech-free time before you get into bed so you can hear your heart.

1. Prayer Upon Waking—*I attuned to the day ahead and invited God's help*

Location_____   *I did this*___(___Minutes) No___

2. As I Lie Down to Sleep—*I offered my heart and dreams to God*

Location_____   *I did this*___(___Minutes) No___

Desolation From the Day – Write no more than two sentences on what decreased *your faith, your hope, and your love for God and neighbor today.*

Consolation From the Day – Write no more than two sentences on what increased *your faith, your hope, and your love for God and neighbor today.*

SPIRITUAL RECORD

For Weeks 1-16, try to spend twenty minutes in the morning and in the evening without technology. When you awake, attune to the day, and offer you day to God with a morning offering. When you go to sleep at night, have a space of tech-free time before you get into bed so you can hear your heart.

1. Prayer Upon Waking—*I attuned to the day ahead and invited God's help*

Location_____   *I did this*___(___Minutes) No___

2. As I Lie Down to Sleep—*I offered my heart and dreams to God*

Location_____   *I did this*___(___Minutes) No___

Desolation From the Day – <u>Write no more than two sentences</u> on what decreased *your faith, your hope, and your love for God and neighbor today.*

Consolation From the Day – <u>Write no more than two sentences</u> on what increased *your faith, your hope, and your love for God and neighbor today.*

SPIRITUAL RECORD

For Weeks 1-16, try to spend twenty minutes in the morning and in the evening without technology. When you awake, attune to the day, and offer you day to God with a morning offering. When you go to sleep at night, have a space of tech-free time before you get into bed so you can hear your heart.

1. Prayer Upon Waking—*I attuned to the day ahead and invited God's help*

Location_____   *I did this*___(___Minutes) No___

2. As I Lie Down to Sleep—*I offered my heart and dreams to God*

Location_____   *I did this*___(___Minutes) No___

Desolation From the Day – <u>Write no more than two sentences</u> on what decreased *your faith, your hope, and your love for God and neighbor today.*

Consolation From the Day – <u>Write no more than two sentences</u> on what increased *your faith, your hope, and your love for God and neighbor today.*

SPIRITUAL RECORD

For Weeks 1-16, try to spend twenty minutes in the morning and in the evening without technology. When you awake, attune to the day, and offer you day to God with a morning offering. When you go to sleep at night, have a space of tech-free time before you get into bed so you can hear your heart.

1. Prayer Upon Waking—*I attuned to the day ahead and invited God's help*

Location_____   *I did this___(___Minutes)* No___

2. As I Lie Down to Sleep—*I offered my heart and dreams to God*

Location_____   *I did this___(___Minutes)* No___

Desolation From the Day – <u>Write no more than two sentences</u> on what decreased *your faith, your hope, and your love for God and neighbor today.*

Consolation From the Day – <u>Write no more than two sentences</u> on what increased *your faith, your hope, and your love for God and neighbor today.*

SPIRITUAL RECORD

For Weeks 1-16, try to spend twenty minutes in the morning and in the evening without technology. When you awake, attune to the day, and offer you day to God with a morning offering. When you go to sleep at night, have a space of tech-free time before you get into bed so you can hear your heart.

1. Prayer Upon Waking—*I attuned to the day ahead and invited God's help*

Location_____   *I did this*___(___Minutes) No___

2. As I Lie Down to Sleep—*I offered my heart and dreams to God*

Location_____   *I did this*___(___Minutes) No___

Desolation From the Day – <u>Write no more than two sentences</u> on what decreased *your faith, your hope, and your love for God and neighbor today.*

Consolation From the Day – <u>Write no more than two sentences</u> on what increased *your faith, your hope, and your love for God and neighbor today.*

 Week 5

For Weeks 1-16, try to spend twenty minutes in the morning and in the evening without technology. When you awake, attune to the day, and offer you day to God with a morning offering. When you go to sleep at night, have a space of tech-free time before you get into bed so you can hear your heart.

1. Prayer Upon Waking—*I attuned to the day ahead and invited God's help*

Location_____ *I did this____(____Minutes) No____*

2. As I Lie Down to Sleep—*I offered my heart and dreams to God*

Location_____ *I did this____(____Minutes) No____*

Desolation From the Day – <u>Write no more than two sentences</u> **on what decreased** *your faith, your hope, and your love for God and neighbor today.*

Consolation From the Day – <u>Write no more than two sentences</u> **on what increased** *your faith, your hope, and your love for God and neighbor today.*

SPIRITUAL RECORD

For Weeks 1-16, try to spend twenty minutes in the morning and in the evening without technology. When you awake, attune to the day, and offer you day to God with a morning offering. When you go to sleep at night, have a space of tech-free time before you get into bed so you can hear your heart.

1. Prayer Upon Waking—*I attuned to the day ahead and invited God's help*

Location_____ *I did this*___(___Minutes) No___

2. As I Lie Down to Sleep—*I offered my heart and dreams to God*

Location_____ *I did this*___(___Minutes) No___

Desolation From the Day – <u>Write no more than two sentences</u> on what decreased *your faith, your hope, and your love for God and neighbor today.*

Consolation From the Day – <u>Write no more than two sentences</u> on what increased *your faith, your hope, and your love for God and neighbor today.*

SPIRITUAL RECORD

For Weeks 1-16, try to spend twenty minutes in the morning and in the evening without technology. When you awake, attune to the day, and offer you day to God with a morning offering. When you go to sleep at night, have a space of tech-free time before you get into bed so you can hear your heart.

1. Prayer Upon Waking—*I attuned to the day ahead and invited God's help*

Location_____   *I did this*___(___Minutes) No___

2. As I Lie Down to Sleep—*I offered my heart and dreams to God*

Location_____   *I did this*___(___Minutes) No___

Desolation From the Day – <u>Write no more than two sentences</u> on what decreased *your faith, your hope, and your love for God and neighbor today.*

Consolation From the Day – <u>Write no more than two sentences</u> on what increased *your faith, your hope, and your love for God and neighbor today.*

SPIRITUAL RECORD

For Weeks 1-16, try to spend twenty minutes in the morning and in the evening without technology. When you awake, attune to the day, and offer you day to God with a morning offering. When you go to sleep at night, have a space of tech-free time before you get into bed so you can hear your heart.

1. Prayer Upon Waking—*I attuned to the day ahead and invited God's help*

Location_____   *I did this*___(___Minutes) No___

2. As I Lie Down to Sleep—*I offered my heart and dreams to God*

Location_____   *I did this*___(___Minutes) No___

Desolation From the Day – <u>Write no more than two sentences</u> on what decreased *your faith, your hope, and your love for God and neighbor today.*

Consolation From the Day – <u>Write no more than two sentences</u> on what increased *your faith, your hope, and your love for God and neighbor today.*

SPIRITUAL RECORD

For Weeks 1-16, try to spend twenty minutes in the morning and in the evening without technology. When you awake, attune to the day, and offer you day to God with a morning offering. When you go to sleep at night, have a space of tech-free time before you get into bed so you can hear your heart.

1. Prayer Upon Waking—*I attuned to the day ahead and invited God's help*

Location_____   *I did this*___(___Minutes) No___

2. As I Lie Down to Sleep—*I offered my heart and dreams to God*

Location_____   *I did this*___(___Minutes) No___

Desolation From the Day – <u>Write no more than two sentences</u> on what decreased *your faith, your hope, and your love for God and neighbor today.*

Consolation From the Day – <u>Write no more than two sentences</u> on what increased *your faith, your hope, and your love for God and neighbor today.*

SPIRITUAL RECORD

For Weeks 1-16, try to spend twenty minutes in the morning and in the evening without technology. When you awake, attune to the day, and offer you day to God with a morning offering. When you go to sleep at night, have a space of tech-free time before you get into bed so you can hear your heart.

1. Prayer Upon Waking—*I attuned to the day ahead and invited God's help*

Location_____ *I did this*___(___Minutes) No___

2. As I Lie Down to Sleep—*I offered my heart and dreams to God*

Location_____ *I did this*___(___Minutes) No___

Desolation From the Day – <u>Write no more than two sentences</u> **on what decreased** *your faith, your hope, and your love for God and neighbor today.*

Consolation From the Day – <u>Write no more than two sentences</u> **on what increased** *your faith, your hope, and your love for God and neighbor today.*

SPIRITUAL RECORD

For Weeks 1-16, try to spend twenty minutes in the morning and in the evening without technology. When you awake, attune to the day, and offer you day to God with a morning offering. When you go to sleep at night, have a space of tech-free time before you get into bed so you can hear your heart.

1. Prayer Upon Waking—*I attuned to the day ahead and invited God's help*

Location_____   *I did this___(___Minutes) No___*

2. As I Lie Down to Sleep—*I offered my heart and dreams to God*

Location_____   *I did this___(___Minutes) No___*

Desolation From the Day – <u>Write no more than two sentences</u> on what decreased *your faith, your hope, and your love for God and neighbor today.*

Consolation From the Day – <u>Write no more than two sentences</u> on what increased *your faith, your hope, and your love for God and neighbor today.*

 Week 6

For Weeks 1-16, try to spend twenty minutes in the morning and in the evening without technology. When you awake, attune to the day, and offer you day to God with a morning offering. When you go to sleep at night, have a space of tech-free time before you get into bed so you can hear your heart.

1. Prayer Upon Waking—*I attuned to the day ahead and invited God's help*

Location_____   *I did this*___(___Minutes) No___

2. As I Lie Down to Sleep—*I offered my heart and dreams to God*

Location_____   *I did this*___(___Minutes) No___

Desolation From the Day – <u>Write no more than two sentences</u> on what decreased *your faith, your hope, and your love for God and neighbor today.*

Consolation From the Day – <u>Write no more than two sentences</u> on what increased *your faith, your hope, and your love for God and neighbor today.*

SPIRITUAL RECORD

For Weeks 1-16, try to spend twenty minutes in the morning and in the evening without technology. When you awake, attune to the day, and offer you day to God with a morning offering. When you go to sleep at night, have a space of tech-free time before you get into bed so you can hear your heart.

1. Prayer Upon Waking—*I attuned to the day ahead and invited God's help*

Location_____ *I did this*___(___Minutes) No___

2. As I Lie Down to Sleep—*I offered my heart and dreams to God*

Location_____ *I did this*___(___Minutes) No___

Desolation From the Day – <u>Write no more than two sentences</u> on what decreased *your faith, your hope, and your love for God and neighbor today.*

Consolation From the Day – <u>Write no more than two sentences</u> on what increased *your faith, your hope, and your love for God and neighbor today.*

SPIRITUAL RECORD

For Weeks 1-16, try to spend twenty minutes in the morning and in the evening without technology. When you awake, attune to the day, and offer you day to God with a morning offering. When you go to sleep at night, have a space of tech-free time before you get into bed so you can hear your heart.

1. Prayer Upon Waking—*I attuned to the day ahead and invited God's help*

Location_____ *I did this*___(___Minutes) No___

2. As I Lie Down to Sleep—*I offered my heart and dreams to God*

Location_____ *I did this*___(___Minutes) No___

Desolation From the Day – <u>Write no more than two sentences</u> on what decreased *your faith, your hope, and your love for God and neighbor today.*

Consolation From the Day – <u>Write no more than two sentences</u> on what increased *your faith, your hope, and your love for God and neighbor today.*

SPIRITUAL RECORD

For Weeks 1-16, try to spend twenty minutes in the morning and in the evening without technology. When you awake, attune to the day, and offer you day to God with a morning offering. When you go to sleep at night, have a space of tech-free time before you get into bed so you can hear your heart.

1. Prayer Upon Waking—*I attuned to the day ahead and invited God's help*

Location_____   *I did this*___(___Minutes) No___

2. As I Lie Down to Sleep—*I offered my heart and dreams to God*

Location_____   *I did this*___(___Minutes) No___

Desolation From the Day – <u>Write no more than two sentences</u> on what decreased *your faith, your hope, and your love for God and neighbor today.*

Consolation From the Day – <u>Write no more than two sentences</u> on what increased *your faith, your hope, and your love for God and neighbor today.*

SPIRITUAL RECORD

For Weeks 1-16, try to spend twenty minutes in the morning and in the evening without technology. When you awake, attune to the day, and offer you day to God with a morning offering. When you go to sleep at night, have a space of tech-free time before you get into bed so you can hear your heart.

1. Prayer Upon Waking—*I attuned to the day ahead and invited God's help*

Location_____   *I did this*___(___Minutes) No___

2. As I Lie Down to Sleep—*I offered my heart and dreams to God*

Location_____   *I did this*___(___Minutes) No___

Desolation From the Day – <u>Write no more than two sentences</u> on what decreased *your faith, your hope, and your love for God and neighbor today.*

Consolation From the Day – <u>Write no more than two sentences</u> on what increased *your faith, your hope, and your love for God and neighbor today.*

SPIRITUAL RECORD

For Weeks 1-16, try to spend twenty minutes in the morning and in the evening without technology. When you awake, attune to the day, and offer you day to God with a morning offering. When you go to sleep at night, have a space of tech-free time before you get into bed so you can hear your heart.

1. Prayer Upon Waking—*I attuned to the day ahead and invited God's help*

Location_____   *I did this*___(___Minutes) No___

2. As I Lie Down to Sleep—*I offered my heart and dreams to God*

Location_____   *I did this*___(___Minutes) No___

Desolation From the Day – <u>Write no more than two sentences</u> on what decreased *your faith, your hope, and your love for God and neighbor today.*

Consolation From the Day – <u>Write no more than two sentences</u> on what increased *your faith, your hope, and your love for God and neighbor today.*

SPIRITUAL RECORD

For Weeks 1-16, try to spend twenty minutes in the morning and in the evening without technology. When you awake, attune to the day, and offer you day to God with a morning offering. When you go to sleep at night, have a space of tech-free time before you get into bed so you can hear your heart.

1. Prayer Upon Waking—*I attuned to the day ahead and invited God's help*

Location_____ *I did this*___(___Minutes) No___

2. As I Lie Down to Sleep—*I offered my heart and dreams to God*

Location_____ *I did this*___(___Minutes) No___

Desolation From the Day – <u>Write no more than two sentences</u> **on what decreased** *your faith, your hope, and your love for God and neighbor today.*

Consolation From the Day – <u>Write no more than two sentences</u> **on what increased** *your faith, your hope, and your love for God and neighbor today.*

Week 7

For Weeks 1-16, try to spend twenty minutes in the morning and in the evening without technology. When you awake, attune to the day, and offer you day to God with a morning offering. When you go to sleep at night, have a space of tech-free time before you get into bed so you can hear your heart.

1. Prayer Upon Waking—*I attuned to the day ahead and invited God's help*

Location_____ *I did this*___(___Minutes) No___

2. As I Lie Down to Sleep—*I offered my heart and dreams to God*

Location_____ *I did this*___(___Minutes) No___

Desolation From the Day – <u>Write no more than two sentences</u> on what decreased *your faith, your hope, and your love for God and neighbor today.*

Consolation From the Day – <u>Write no more than two sentences</u> on what increased *your faith, your hope, and your love for God and neighbor today.*

SPIRITUAL RECORD

For Weeks 1-16, try to spend twenty minutes in the morning and in the evening without technology. When you awake, attune to the day, and offer you day to God with a morning offering. When you go to sleep at night, have a space of tech-free time before you get into bed so you can hear your heart.

1. Prayer Upon Waking—*I attuned to the day ahead and invited God's help*

Location_____   *I did this*___(___Minutes) No___

2. As I Lie Down to Sleep—*I offered my heart and dreams to God*

Location_____   *I did this*___(___Minutes) No___

Desolation From the Day – <u>Write no more than two sentences</u> on what decreased *your faith, your hope, and your love for God and neighbor today.*

Consolation From the Day – <u>Write no more than two sentences</u> on what increased *your faith, your hope, and your love for God and neighbor today.*

SPIRITUAL RECORD

For Weeks 1-16, try to spend twenty minutes in the morning and in the evening without technology. When you awake, attune to the day, and offer you day to God with a morning offering. When you go to sleep at night, have a space of tech-free time before you get into bed so you can hear your heart.

1. Prayer Upon Waking—*I attuned to the day ahead and invited God's help*

Location_____   *I did this*___(___Minutes) No___

2. As I Lie Down to Sleep—*I offered my heart and dreams to God*

Location_____   *I did this*___(___Minutes) No___

Desolation From the Day – <u>Write no more than two sentences</u> on what decreased *your faith, your hope, and your love for God and neighbor today.*

Consolation From the Day – <u>Write no more than two sentences</u> on what increased *your faith, your hope, and your love for God and neighbor today.*

SPIRITUAL RECORD

For Weeks 1-16, try to spend twenty minutes in the morning and in the evening without technology. When you awake, attune to the day, and offer you day to God with a morning offering. When you go to sleep at night, have a space of tech-free time before you get into bed so you can hear your heart.

1. Prayer Upon Waking—*I attuned to the day ahead and invited God's help*

Location_____   *I did this*___(___Minutes) No___

2. As I Lie Down to Sleep—*I offered my heart and dreams to God*

Location_____   *I did this*___(___Minutes) No___

Desolation From the Day – <u>Write no more than two sentences</u> on what decreased *your faith, your hope, and your love for God and neighbor today.*

Consolation From the Day – <u>Write no more than two sentences</u> on what increased *your faith, your hope, and your love for God and neighbor today.*

SPIRITUAL RECORD

For Weeks 1-16, try to spend twenty minutes in the morning and in the evening without technology. When you awake, attune to the day, and offer you day to God with a morning offering. When you go to sleep at night, have a space of tech-free time before you get into bed so you can hear your heart.

1. Prayer Upon Waking—*I attuned to the day ahead and invited God's help*

Location_____ *I did this*___(___Minutes) No___

2. As I Lie Down to Sleep—*I offered my heart and dreams to God*

Location_____ *I did this*___(___Minutes) No___

Desolation From the Day – <u>Write no more than two sentences</u> on what decreased *your faith, your hope, and your love for God and neighbor today.*

Consolation From the Day – <u>Write no more than two sentences</u> on what increased *your faith, your hope, and your love for God and neighbor today.*

SPIRITUAL RECORD

For Weeks 1-16, try to spend twenty minutes in the morning and in the evening without technology. When you awake, attune to the day, and offer you day to God with a morning offering. When you go to sleep at night, have a space of tech-free time before you get into bed so you can hear your heart.

1. Prayer Upon Waking—*I attuned to the day ahead and invited God's help*

Location_____   *I did this*___(___Minutes) No___

2. As I Lie Down to Sleep—*I offered my heart and dreams to God*

Location_____   *I did this*___(___Minutes) No___

Desolation From the Day – <u>Write no more than two sentences</u> on what decreased *your faith, your hope, and your love for God and neighbor today.*

Consolation From the Day – <u>Write no more than two sentences</u> on what increased *your faith, your hope, and your love for God and neighbor today.*

SPIRITUAL RECORD

For Weeks 1-16, try to spend twenty minutes in the morning and in the evening without technology. When you awake, attune to the day, and offer you day to God with a morning offering. When you go to sleep at night, have a space of tech-free time before you get into bed so you can hear your heart.

1. Prayer Upon Waking—*I attuned to the day ahead and invited God's help*

Location_____ *I did this*___(___Minutes) No___

2. As I Lie Down to Sleep—*I offered my heart and dreams to God*

Location_____ *I did this*___(___Minutes) No___

Desolation From the Day – <u>Write no more than two sentences</u> **on what decreased *your faith, your hope, and your love for God and neighbor today.***

Consolation From the Day – <u>Write no more than two sentences</u> **on what increased *your faith, your hope, and your love for God and neighbor today.***

 # Week 8

For Weeks 1-16, try to spend twenty minutes in the morning and in the evening without technology. When you awake, attune to the day, and offer you day to God with a morning offering. When you go to sleep at night, have a space of tech-free time before you get into bed so you can hear your heart.

1. Prayer Upon Waking—*I attuned to the day ahead and invited God's help*

Location_____   *I did this___(___Minutes)* No___

2. As I Lie Down to Sleep—*I offered my heart and dreams to God*

Location_____   *I did this___(___Minutes)* No___

Desolation From the Day – <u>Write no more than two sentences</u> on what decreased *your faith, your hope, and your love for God and neighbor today.*

Consolation From the Day – <u>Write no more than two sentences</u> on what increased *your faith, your hope, and your love for God and neighbor today.*

SPIRITUAL RECORD

For Weeks 1-16, try to spend twenty minutes in the morning and in the evening without technology. When you awake, attune to the day, and offer you day to God with a morning offering. When you go to sleep at night, have a space of tech-free time before you get into bed so you can hear your heart.

1. Prayer Upon Waking—*I attuned to the day ahead and invited God's help*

Location_____   *I did this___(___Minutes) No___*

2. As I Lie Down to Sleep—*I offered my heart and dreams to God*

Location_____   *I did this___(___Minutes) No___*

Desolation From the Day – <u>Write no more than two sentences</u> on what decreased *your faith, your hope, and your love for God and neighbor today.*

Consolation From the Day – <u>Write no more than two sentences</u> on what increased *your faith, your hope, and your love for God and neighbor today.*

SPIRITUAL RECORD

For Weeks 1-16, try to spend twenty minutes in the morning and in the evening without technology. When you awake, attune to the day, and offer you day to God with a morning offering. When you go to sleep at night, have a space of tech-free time before you get into bed so you can hear your heart.

1. Prayer Upon Waking—_I attuned to the day ahead and invited God's help_

Location_____ _I did this___(___Minutes) No___

2. As I Lie Down to Sleep—_I offered my heart and dreams to God_

Location_____ _I did this___(___Minutes) No___

Desolation From the Day – <u>Write no more than two sentences</u> on what decreased _your faith, your hope, and your love for God and neighbor today._

Consolation From the Day – <u>Write no more than two sentences</u> on what increased _your faith, your hope, and your love for God and neighbor today._

SPIRITUAL RECORD

For Weeks 1-16, try to spend twenty minutes in the morning and in the evening without technology. When you awake, attune to the day, and offer you day to God with a morning offering. When you go to sleep at night, have a space of tech-free time before you get into bed so you can hear your heart.

1. Prayer Upon Waking—*I attuned to the day ahead and invited God's help*

Location_____   *I did this*___(___Minutes) No___

2. As I Lie Down to Sleep—*I offered my heart and dreams to God*

Location_____   *I did this*___(___Minutes) No___

Desolation From the Day – <u>Write no more than two sentences</u> **on what decreased** *your faith, your hope, and your love for God and neighbor today.*

Consolation From the Day – <u>Write no more than two sentences</u> **on what increased** *your faith, your hope, and your love for God and neighbor today.*

SPIRITUAL RECORD

For Weeks 1-16, try to spend twenty minutes in the morning and in the evening without technology. When you awake, attune to the day, and offer you day to God with a morning offering. When you go to sleep at night, have a space of tech-free time before you get into bed so you can hear your heart.

1. Prayer Upon Waking—*I attuned to the day ahead and invited God's help*

Location_____   *I did this___(___Minutes)* No___

2. As I Lie Down to Sleep—*I offered my heart and dreams to God*

Location_____   *I did this___(___Minutes)* No___

Desolation From the Day – <u>Write no more than two sentences</u> on what decreased *your faith, your hope, and your love for God and neighbor today.*

Consolation From the Day – <u>Write no more than two sentences</u> on what increased *your faith, your hope, and your love for God and neighbor today.*

SPIRITUAL RECORD

For Weeks 1-16, try to spend twenty minutes in the morning and in the evening without technology. When you awake, attune to the day, and offer you day to God with a morning offering. When you go to sleep at night, have a space of tech-free time before you get into bed so you can hear your heart.

1. Prayer Upon Waking—*I attuned to the day ahead and invited God's help*

Location_____ *I did this*___(___Minutes) No___

2. As I Lie Down to Sleep—*I offered my heart and dreams to God*

Location_____ *I did this*___(___Minutes) No___

Desolation From the Day – <u>Write no more than two sentences</u> on what decreased *your faith, your hope, and your love for God and neighbor today.*

Consolation From the Day – <u>Write no more than two sentences</u> on what increased *your faith, your hope, and your love for God and neighbor today.*

SPIRITUAL RECORD

For Weeks 1-16, try to spend twenty minutes in the morning and in the evening without technology. When you awake, attune to the day, and offer you day to God with a morning offering. When you go to sleep at night, have a space of tech-free time before you get into bed so you can hear your heart.

1. Prayer Upon Waking—*I attuned to the day ahead and invited God's help*

Location_____ *I did this*___(___Minutes) No___

2. As I Lie Down to Sleep—*I offered my heart and dreams to God*

Location_____ *I did this*___(___Minutes) No___

Desolation From the Day – <u>Write no more than two sentences</u> on what decreased *your faith, your hope, and your love for God and neighbor today.*

Consolation From the Day – <u>Write no more than two sentences</u> on what increased *your faith, your hope, and your love for God and neighbor today.*

 # Week 9

For Weeks 1-16, try to spend twenty minutes in the morning and in the evening without technology. When you awake, attune to the day, and offer you day to God with a morning offering. When you go to sleep at night, have a space of tech-free time before you get into bed so you can hear your heart.

1. Prayer Upon Waking—*I attuned to the day ahead and invited God's help*

Location_____   *I did this*___(___Minutes) No___

2. As I Lie Down to Sleep—*I offered my heart and dreams to God*

Location_____   *I did this*___(___Minutes) No___

Desolation From the Day – <u>Write no more than two sentences</u> on what decreased *your faith, your hope, and your love for God and neighbor today.*

Consolation From the Day – <u>Write no more than two sentences</u> on what increased *your faith, your hope, and your love for God and neighbor today.*

SPIRITUAL RECORD

For Weeks 1-16, try to spend twenty minutes in the morning and in the evening without technology. When you awake, attune to the day, and offer you day to God with a morning offering. When you go to sleep at night, have a space of tech-free time before you get into bed so you can hear your heart.

1. Prayer Upon Waking—*I attuned to the day ahead and invited God's help*

Location_____   *I did this*___(___Minutes) No___

2. As I Lie Down to Sleep—*I offered my heart and dreams to God*

Location_____   *I did this*___(___Minutes) No___

Desolation From the Day – <u>Write no more than two sentences</u> on what decreased *your faith, your hope, and your love for God and neighbor today.*

Consolation From the Day – <u>Write no more than two sentences</u> on what increased *your faith, your hope, and your love for God and neighbor today.*

SPIRITUAL RECORD

For Weeks 1-16, try to spend twenty minutes in the morning and in the evening without technology. When you awake, attune to the day, and offer you day to God with a morning offering. When you go to sleep at night, have a space of tech-free time before you get into bed so you can hear your heart.

1. Prayer Upon Waking—*I attuned to the day ahead and invited God's help*

Location_____   *I did this___(___Minutes)* No___

2. As I Lie Down to Sleep—*I offered my heart and dreams to God*

Location_____   *I did this___(___Minutes)* No___

Desolation From the Day – <u>Write no more than two sentences</u> on what decreased *your faith, your hope, and your love for God and neighbor today.*

Consolation From the Day – <u>Write no more than two sentences</u> on what increased *your faith, your hope, and your love for God and neighbor today.*

SPIRITUAL RECORD

For Weeks 1-16, try to spend twenty minutes in the morning and in the evening without technology. When you awake, attune to the day, and offer you day to God with a morning offering. When you go to sleep at night, have a space of tech-free time before you get into bed so you can hear your heart.

1. Prayer Upon Waking—*I attuned to the day ahead and invited God's help*

Location_____   *I did this___(___Minutes) No___*

2. As I Lie Down to Sleep—*I offered my heart and dreams to God*

Location_____   *I did this___(___Minutes) No___*

Desolation From the Day – <u>Write no more than two sentences</u> on what decreased *your faith, your hope, and your love for God and neighbor today.*

Consolation From the Day – <u>Write no more than two sentences</u> on what increased *your faith, your hope, and your love for God and neighbor today.*

SPIRITUAL RECORD

For Weeks 1-16, try to spend twenty minutes in the morning and in the evening without technology. When you awake, attune to the day, and offer you day to God with a morning offering. When you go to sleep at night, have a space of tech-free time before you get into bed so you can hear your heart.

1. Prayer Upon Waking—*I attuned to the day ahead and invited God's help*

Location_____   *I did this*___(___Minutes) No___

2. As I Lie Down to Sleep—*I offered my heart and dreams to God*

Location_____   *I did this*___(___Minutes) No___

Desolation From the Day – <u>Write no more than two sentences</u> on what decreased *your faith, your hope, and your love for God and neighbor today.*

Consolation From the Day – <u>Write no more than two sentences</u> on what increased *your faith, your hope, and your love for God and neighbor today.*

SPIRITUAL RECORD

For Weeks 1-16, try to spend twenty minutes in the morning and in the evening without technology. When you awake, attune to the day, and offer you day to God with a morning offering. When you go to sleep at night, have a space of tech-free time before you get into bed so you can hear your heart.

1. Prayer Upon Waking—*I attuned to the day ahead and invited God's help*

Location_____ *I did this*___(___Minutes) No___

2. As I Lie Down to Sleep—*I offered my heart and dreams to God*

Location_____ *I did this*___(___Minutes) No___

Desolation From the Day – <u>Write no more than two sentences</u> on what decreased *your faith, your hope, and your love for God and neighbor today.*

Consolation From the Day – <u>Write no more than two sentences</u> on what increased *your faith, your hope, and your love for God and neighbor today.*

SPIRITUAL RECORD

For Weeks 1-16, try to spend twenty minutes in the morning and in the evening without technology. When you awake, attune to the day, and offer you day to God with a morning offering. When you go to sleep at night, have a space of tech-free time before you get into bed so you can hear your heart.

1. Prayer Upon Waking—*I attuned to the day ahead and invited God's help*

Location_____   *I did this___(___Minutes) No___*

2. As I Lie Down to Sleep—*I offered my heart and dreams to God*

Location_____   *I did this___(___Minutes) No___*

Desolation From the Day – <u>Write no more than two sentences</u> on what decreased *your faith, your hope, and your love for God and neighbor today.*

Consolation From the Day – <u>Write no more than two sentences</u> on what increased *your faith, your hope, and your love for God and neighbor today.*

Week 10

For Weeks 1-16, try to spend twenty minutes in the morning and in the evening without technology. When you awake, attune to the day, and offer you day to God with a morning offering. When you go to sleep at night, have a space of tech-free time before you get into bed so you can hear your heart.

1. Prayer Upon Waking—*I attuned to the day ahead and invited God's help*

Location_____ *I did this*___(___Minutes) No___

2. As I Lie Down to Sleep—*I offered my heart and dreams to God*

Location_____ *I did this*___(___Minutes) No___

Desolation From the Day – <u>Write no more than two sentences</u> on what decreased *your faith, your hope, and your love for God and neighbor today.*

Consolation From the Day – <u>Write no more than two sentences</u> on what increased *your faith, your hope, and your love for God and neighbor today.*

SPIRITUAL RECORD

For Weeks 1-16, try to spend twenty minutes in the morning and in the evening without technology. When you awake, attune to the day, and offer you day to God with a morning offering. When you go to sleep at night, have a space of tech-free time before you get into bed so you can hear your heart.

1. Prayer Upon Waking—*I attuned to the day ahead and invited God's help*

Location_____   *I did this*___(___Minutes) No___

2. As I Lie Down to Sleep—*I offered my heart and dreams to God*

Location_____   *I did this*___(___Minutes) No___

Desolation From the Day – <u>Write no more than two sentences</u> on what decreased *your faith, your hope, and your love for God and neighbor today.*

Consolation From the Day – <u>Write no more than two sentences</u> on what increased *your faith, your hope, and your love for God and neighbor today.*

SPIRITUAL RECORD

For Weeks 1-16, try to spend twenty minutes in the morning and in the evening without technology. When you awake, attune to the day, and offer you day to God with a morning offering. When you go to sleep at night, have a space of tech-free time before you get into bed so you can hear your heart.

1. Prayer Upon Waking—*I attuned to the day ahead and invited God's help*

Location_____   *I did this*___(___Minutes) No___

2. As I Lie Down to Sleep—*I offered my heart and dreams to God*

Location_____   *I did this*___(___Minutes) No___

Desolation From the Day – <u>Write no more than two sentences</u> on what decreased *your faith, your hope, and your love for God and neighbor today.*

Consolation From the Day – <u>Write no more than two sentences</u> on what increased *your faith, your hope, and your love for God and neighbor today.*

SPIRITUAL RECORD

For Weeks 1-16, try to spend twenty minutes in the morning and in the evening without technology. When you awake, attune to the day, and offer you day to God with a morning offering. When you go to sleep at night, have a space of tech-free time before you get into bed so you can hear your heart.

1. Prayer Upon Waking—*I attuned to the day ahead and invited God's help*

Location_____ *I did this*___(___Minutes) No___

2. As I Lie Down to Sleep—*I offered my heart and dreams to God*

Location_____ *I did this*___(___Minutes) No___

Desolation From the Day – <u>Write no more than two sentences</u> on what decreased *your faith, your hope, and your love for God and neighbor today.*

Consolation From the Day – <u>Write no more than two sentences</u> on what increased *your faith, your hope, and your love for God and neighbor today.*

SPIRITUAL RECORD

For Weeks 1-16, try to spend twenty minutes in the morning and in the evening without technology. When you awake, attune to the day, and offer you day to God with a morning offering. When you go to sleep at night, have a space of tech-free time before you get into bed so you can hear your heart.

1. Prayer Upon Waking—*I attuned to the day ahead and invited God's help*

Location_____   *I did this*___(___Minutes) No___

2. As I Lie Down to Sleep—*I offered my heart and dreams to God*

Location_____   *I did this*___(___Minutes) No___

Desolation From the Day – <u>Write no more than two sentences</u> on what decreased *your faith, your hope, and your love for God and neighbor today.*

Consolation From the Day – <u>Write no more than two sentences</u> on what increased *your faith, your hope, and your love for God and neighbor today.*

SPIRITUAL RECORD

For Weeks 1-16, try to spend twenty minutes in the morning and in the evening without technology. When you awake, attune to the day, and offer you day to God with a morning offering. When you go to sleep at night, have a space of tech-free time before you get into bed so you can hear your heart.

1. Prayer Upon Waking—*I attuned to the day ahead and invited God's help*

Location_____   *I did this*___(___Minutes) No___

2. As I Lie Down to Sleep—*I offered my heart and dreams to God*

Location_____   *I did this*___(___Minutes) No___

Desolation From the Day – <u>Write no more than two sentences</u> on what decreased *your faith, your hope, and your love for God and neighbor today.*

Consolation From the Day – <u>Write no more than two sentences</u> on what increased *your faith, your hope, and your love for God and neighbor today.*

SPIRITUAL RECORD

For Weeks 1-16, try to spend twenty minutes in the morning and in the evening without technology. When you awake, attune to the day, and offer you day to God with a morning offering. When you go to sleep at night, have a space of tech-free time before you get into bed so you can hear your heart.

1. Prayer Upon Waking—*I attuned to the day ahead and invited God's help*

Location_____ *I did this*___(___Minutes) No___

2. As I Lie Down to Sleep—*I offered my heart and dreams to God*

Location_____ *I did this*___(___Minutes) No___

Desolation From the Day – <u>Write no more than two sentences</u> on what decreased *your faith, your hope, and your love for God and neighbor today.*

Consolation From the Day – <u>Write no more than two sentences</u> on what increased *your faith, your hope, and your love for God and neighbor today.*

 # Week 11

For Weeks 1-16, try to spend twenty minutes in the morning and in the evening without technology. When you awake, attune to the day, and offer you day to God with a morning offering. When you go to sleep at night, have a space of tech-free time before you get into bed so you can hear your heart.

1. Prayer Upon Waking—*I attuned to the day ahead and invited God's help*

Location_____ *I did this___(___Minutes) No___*

2. As I Lie Down to Sleep—*I offered my heart and dreams to God*

Location_____ *I did this___(___Minutes) No___*

Desolation From the Day – <u>Write no more than two sentences</u> on what decreased *your faith, your hope, and your love for God and neighbor today.*

Consolation From the Day – <u>Write no more than two sentences</u> on what increased *your faith, your hope, and your love for God and neighbor today.*

SPIRITUAL RECORD

For Weeks 1-16, try to spend twenty minutes in the morning and in the evening without technology. When you awake, attune to the day, and offer you day to God with a morning offering. When you go to sleep at night, have a space of tech-free time before you get into bed so you can hear your heart.

1. Prayer Upon Waking—*I attuned to the day ahead and invited God's help*

Location_____   *I did this*___(___Minutes) No___

2. As I Lie Down to Sleep—*I offered my heart and dreams to God*

Location_____   *I did this*___(___Minutes) No___

Desolation From the Day – <u>Write no more than two sentences</u> on what decreased *your faith, your hope, and your love for God and neighbor today.*

Consolation From the Day – <u>Write no more than two sentences</u> on what increased *your faith, your hope, and your love for God and neighbor today.*

SPIRITUAL RECORD

For Weeks 1-16, try to spend twenty minutes in the morning and in the evening without technology. When you awake, attune to the day, and offer you day to God with a morning offering. When you go to sleep at night, have a space of tech-free time before you get into bed so you can hear your heart.

1. Prayer Upon Waking—*I attuned to the day ahead and invited God's help*

Location_____ *I did this*____(____Minutes) No____

2. As I Lie Down to Sleep—*I offered my heart and dreams to God*

Location_____ *I did this*____(____Minutes) No____

Desolation From the Day – <u>Write no more than two sentences</u> on what decreased *your faith, your hope, and your love for God and neighbor today.*

Consolation From the Day – <u>Write no more than two sentences</u> on what increased *your faith, your hope, and your love for God and neighbor today.*

SPIRITUAL RECORD

For Weeks 1-16, try to spend twenty minutes in the morning and in the evening without technology. When you awake, attune to the day, and offer you day to God with a morning offering. When you go to sleep at night, have a space of tech-free time before you get into bed so you can hear your heart.

1. Prayer Upon Waking—*I attuned to the day ahead and invited God's help*

Location_____   *I did this*___(___Minutes) No___

2. As I Lie Down to Sleep—*I offered my heart and dreams to God*

Location_____   *I did this*___(___Minutes) No___

Desolation From the Day – <u>Write no more than two sentences</u> on what decreased *your faith, your hope, and your love for God and neighbor today.*

Consolation From the Day – <u>Write no more than two sentences</u> on what increased *your faith, your hope, and your love for God and neighbor today.*

SPIRITUAL RECORD

For Weeks 1-16, try to spend twenty minutes in the morning and in the evening without technology. When you awake, attune to the day, and offer you day to God with a morning offering. When you go to sleep at night, have a space of tech-free time before you get into bed so you can hear your heart.

1. Prayer Upon Waking—*I attuned to the day ahead and invited God's help*

Location_____   *I did this*___(___Minutes) No___

2. As I Lie Down to Sleep—*I offered my heart and dreams to God*

Location_____   *I did this*___(___Minutes) No___

Desolation From the Day – <u>Write no more than two sentences</u> on what decreased *your faith, your hope, and your love for God and neighbor today.*

Consolation From the Day – <u>Write no more than two sentences</u> on what increased *your faith, your hope, and your love for God and neighbor today.*

SPIRITUAL RECORD

For Weeks 1-16, try to spend twenty minutes in the morning and in the evening without technology. When you awake, attune to the day, and offer you day to God with a morning offering. When you go to sleep at night, have a space of tech-free time before you get into bed so you can hear your heart.

1. Prayer Upon Waking—*I attuned to the day ahead and invited God's help*

Location_____   *I did this*___(___Minutes) No___

2. As I Lie Down to Sleep—*I offered my heart and dreams to God*

Location_____   *I did this*___(___Minutes) No___

Desolation From the Day – <u>Write no more than two sentences</u> on what decreased *your faith, your hope, and your love for God and neighbor today.*

Consolation From the Day – <u>Write no more than two sentences</u> on what increased *your faith, your hope, and your love for God and neighbor today.*

SPIRITUAL RECORD

For Weeks 1-16, try to spend twenty minutes in the morning and in the evening without technology. When you awake, attune to the day, and offer you day to God with a morning offering. When you go to sleep at night, have a space of tech-free time before you get into bed so you can hear your heart.

1. Prayer Upon Waking—*I attuned to the day ahead and invited God's help*

Location_____ *I did this*___(___Minutes) No___

2. As I Lie Down to Sleep—*I offered my heart and dreams to God*

Location_____ *I did this*___(___Minutes) No___

Desolation From the Day – <u>Write no more than two sentences</u> on what decreased *your faith, your hope, and your love for God and neighbor today.*

Consolation From the Day – <u>Write no more than two sentences</u> on what increased *your faith, your hope, and your love for God and neighbor today.*

 Week 12

For Weeks 1-16, try to spend twenty minutes in the morning and in the evening without technology. When you awake, attune to the day, and offer you day to God with a morning offering. When you go to sleep at night, have a space of tech-free time before you get into bed so you can hear your heart.

1. Prayer Upon Waking—*I attuned to the day ahead and invited God's help*

Location_____ *I did this___(___Minutes) No___*

2. As I Lie Down to Sleep—*I offered my heart and dreams to God*

Location_____ *I did this___(___Minutes) No___*

Desolation From the Day – <u>Write no more than two sentences</u> on what decreased *your faith, your hope, and your love for God and neighbor today.*

Consolation From the Day – <u>Write no more than two sentences</u> on what increased *your faith, your hope, and your love for God and neighbor today.*

SPIRITUAL RECORD

For Weeks 1-16, try to spend twenty minutes in the morning and in the evening without technology. When you awake, attune to the day, and offer you day to God with a morning offering. When you go to sleep at night, have a space of tech-free time before you get into bed so you can hear your heart.

1. Prayer Upon Waking—*I attuned to the day ahead and invited God's help*

Location_____ *I did this___(___Minutes) No___

2. As I Lie Down to Sleep—*I offered my heart and dreams to God*

Location_____ *I did this___(___Minutes) No___

Desolation From the Day – Write no more than two sentences on what decreased *your faith, your hope, and your love for God and neighbor today.*

Consolation From the Day – Write no more than two sentences on what increased *your faith, your hope, and your love for God and neighbor today.*

SPIRITUAL RECORD

For Weeks 1-16, try to spend twenty minutes in the morning and in the evening without technology. When you awake, attune to the day, and offer you day to God with a morning offering. When you go to sleep at night, have a space of tech-free time before you get into bed so you can hear your heart.

1. Prayer Upon Waking—*I attuned to the day ahead and invited God's help*

Location_____   *I did this*___(___Minutes) No___

2. As I Lie Down to Sleep—*I offered my heart and dreams to God*

Location_____   *I did this*___(___Minutes) No___

Desolation From the Day – <u>Write no more than two sentences</u> on what decreased *your faith, your hope, and your love for God and neighbor today.*

Consolation From the Day – <u>Write no more than two sentences</u> on what increased *your faith, your hope, and your love for God and neighbor today.*

SPIRITUAL RECORD

For Weeks 1-16, try to spend twenty minutes in the morning and in the evening without technology. When you awake, attune to the day, and offer you day to God with a morning offering. When you go to sleep at night, have a space of tech-free time before you get into bed so you can hear your heart.

1. Prayer Upon Waking—*I attuned to the day ahead and invited God's help*

Location_____ *I did this*___(___Minutes) No___

2. As I Lie Down to Sleep—*I offered my heart and dreams to God*

Location_____ *I did this*___(___Minutes) No___

Desolation From the Day – <u>Write no more than two sentences</u> on what decreased *your faith, your hope, and your love for God and neighbor today.*

Consolation From the Day – <u>Write no more than two sentences</u> on what increased *your faith, your hope, and your love for God and neighbor today.*

SPIRITUAL RECORD

For Weeks 1-16, try to spend twenty minutes in the morning and in the evening without technology. When you awake, attune to the day, and offer you day to God with a morning offering. When you go to sleep at night, have a space of tech-free time before you get into bed so you can hear your heart.

1. Prayer Upon Waking—*I attuned to the day ahead and invited God's help*

Location_____ *I did this___(___Minutes)* No___

2. As I Lie Down to Sleep—*I offered my heart and dreams to God*

Location_____ *I did this___(___Minutes)* No___

Desolation From the Day – <u>Write no more than two sentences</u> on what decreased *your faith, your hope, and your love for God and neighbor today.*

Consolation From the Day – <u>Write no more than two sentences</u> on what increased *your faith, your hope, and your love for God and neighbor today.*

SPIRITUAL RECORD

For Weeks 1-16, try to spend twenty minutes in the morning and in the evening without technology. When you awake, attune to the day, and offer you day to God with a morning offering. When you go to sleep at night, have a space of tech-free time before you get into bed so you can hear your heart.

1. Prayer Upon Waking—*I attuned to the day ahead and invited God's help*

Location_____   *I did this*___(___Minutes) No___

2. As I Lie Down to Sleep—*I offered my heart and dreams to God*

Location_____   *I did this*___(___Minutes) No___

Desolation From the Day – <u>Write no more than two sentences</u> on what decreased *your faith, your hope, and your love for God and neighbor today.*

Consolation From the Day – <u>Write no more than two sentences</u> on what increased *your faith, your hope, and your love for God and neighbor today.*

SPIRITUAL RECORD

For Weeks 1-16, try to spend twenty minutes in the morning and in the evening without technology. When you awake, attune to the day, and offer you day to God with a morning offering. When you go to sleep at night, have a space of tech-free time before you get into bed so you can hear your heart.

1. Prayer Upon Waking—*I attuned to the day ahead and invited God's help*

Location_____ *I did this*___(___Minutes) No___

2. As I Lie Down to Sleep—*I offered my heart and dreams to God*

Location_____ *I did this*___(___Minutes) No___

**Desolation From the Day – ** <u>Write no more than two sentences</u> on what decreased *your faith, your hope, and your love for God and neighbor today.*

**Consolation From the Day – ** <u>Write no more than two sentences</u> on what increased *your faith, your hope, and your love for God and neighbor today.*

 # Week 13

For Weeks 1-16, try to spend twenty minutes in the morning and in the evening without technology. When you awake, attune to the day, and offer you day to God with a morning offering. When you go to sleep at night, have a space of tech-free time before you get into bed so you can hear your heart.

1. Prayer Upon Waking—*I attuned to the day ahead and invited God's help*

Location_____ *I did this*___(___Minutes) No___

2. As I Lie Down to Sleep—*I offered my heart and dreams to God*

Location_____ *I did this*___(___Minutes) No___

Desolation From the Day – <u>Write no more than two sentences</u> on what decreased *your faith, your hope, and your love for God and neighbor today.*

Consolation From the Day – <u>Write no more than two sentences</u> on what increased *your faith, your hope, and your love for God and neighbor today.*

SPIRITUAL RECORD

For Weeks 1-16, try to spend twenty minutes in the morning and in the evening without technology. When you awake, attune to the day, and offer you day to God with a morning offering. When you go to sleep at night, have a space of tech-free time before you get into bed so you can hear your heart.

1. Prayer Upon Waking—*I attuned to the day ahead and invited God's help*

Location_____   *I did this*___(___Minutes) No___

2. As I Lie Down to Sleep—*I offered my heart and dreams to God*

Location_____   *I did this*___(___Minutes) No___

Desolation From the Day – <u>Write no more than two sentences</u> on what decreased *your faith, your hope, and your love for God and neighbor today.*

Consolation From the Day – <u>Write no more than two sentences</u> on what increased *your faith, your hope, and your love for God and neighbor today.*

SPIRITUAL RECORD

For Weeks 1-16, try to spend twenty minutes in the morning and in the evening without technology. When you awake, attune to the day, and offer you day to God with a morning offering. When you go to sleep at night, have a space of tech-free time before you get into bed so you can hear your heart.

1. Prayer Upon Waking—*I attuned to the day ahead and invited God's help*

Location_____ *I did this*___(___Minutes) No___

2. As I Lie Down to Sleep—*I offered my heart and dreams to God*

Location_____ *I did this*___(___Minutes) No___

Desolation From the Day – <u>Write no more than two sentences</u> on what decreased *your faith, your hope, and your love for God and neighbor today.*

Consolation From the Day – <u>Write no more than two sentences</u> on what increased *your faith, your hope, and your love for God and neighbor today.*

SPIRITUAL RECORD

For Weeks 1-16, try to spend twenty minutes in the morning and in the evening without technology. When you awake, attune to the day, and offer you day to God with a morning offering. When you go to sleep at night, have a space of tech-free time before you get into bed so you can hear your heart.

1. Prayer Upon Waking—*I attuned to the day ahead and invited God's help*

Location_____   *I did this*___(___Minutes) No___

2. As I Lie Down to Sleep—*I offered my heart and dreams to God*

Location_____   *I did this*___(___Minutes) No___

Desolation From the Day – <u>Write no more than two sentences</u> on what decreased *your faith, your hope, and your love for God and neighbor today.*

Consolation From the Day – <u>Write no more than two sentences</u> on what increased *your faith, your hope, and your love for God and neighbor today.*

SPIRITUAL RECORD

For Weeks 1-16, try to spend twenty minutes in the morning and in the evening without technology. When you awake, attune to the day, and offer you day to God with a morning offering. When you go to sleep at night, have a space of tech-free time before you get into bed so you can hear your heart.

1. Prayer Upon Waking—*I attuned to the day ahead and invited God's help*

Location_____ *I did this*___(___Minutes) No___

2. As I Lie Down to Sleep—*I offered my heart and dreams to God*

Location_____ *I did this*___(___Minutes) No___

Desolation From the Day – <u>Write no more than two sentences</u> **on what decreased** *your faith, your hope, and your love for God and neighbor today.*

Consolation From the Day – <u>Write no more than two sentences</u> **on what increased** *your faith, your hope, and your love for God and neighbor today.*

SPIRITUAL RECORD

For Weeks 1-16, try to spend twenty minutes in the morning and in the evening without technology. When you awake, attune to the day, and offer you day to God with a morning offering. When you go to sleep at night, have a space of tech-free time before you get into bed so you can hear your heart.

1. Prayer Upon Waking—*I attuned to the day ahead and invited God's help*

Location_____ *I did this*___(___Minutes) No___

2. As I Lie Down to Sleep—*I offered my heart and dreams to God*

Location_____ *I did this*___(___Minutes) No___

Desolation From the Day – <u>Write no more than two sentences</u> on what decreased *your faith, your hope, and your love for God and neighbor today.*

Consolation From the Day – <u>Write no more than two sentences</u> on what increased *your faith, your hope, and your love for God and neighbor today.*

SPIRITUAL RECORD

For Weeks 1-16, try to spend twenty minutes in the morning and in the evening without technology. When you awake, attune to the day, and offer you day to God with a morning offering. When you go to sleep at night, have a space of tech-free time before you get into bed so you can hear your heart.

1. Prayer Upon Waking—*I attuned to the day ahead and invited God's help*

Location_____   *I did this___(___Minutes)* No___

2. As I Lie Down to Sleep—*I offered my heart and dreams to God*

Location_____   *I did this___(___Minutes)* No___

Desolation From the Day – <u>Write no more than two sentences</u> on what decreased *your faith, your hope, and your love for God and neighbor today.*

Consolation From the Day – <u>Write no more than two sentences</u> on what increased *your faith, your hope, and your love for God and neighbor today.*

Week 14

For Weeks 1-16, try to spend twenty minutes in the morning and in the evening without technology. When you awake, attune to the day, and offer you day to God with a morning offering. When you go to sleep at night, have a space of tech-free time before you get into bed so you can hear your heart.

1. Prayer Upon Waking—*I attuned to the day ahead and invited God's help*

Location_____ *I did this*___(___Minutes) No___

2. As I Lie Down to Sleep—*I offered my heart and dreams to God*

Location_____ *I did this*___(___Minutes) No___

Desolation From the Day – <u>Write no more than two sentences</u> on what decreased *your faith, your hope, and your love for God and neighbor today.*

Consolation From the Day – <u>Write no more than two sentences</u> on what increased *your faith, your hope, and your love for God and neighbor today.*

SPIRITUAL RECORD

For Weeks 1-16, try to spend twenty minutes in the morning and in the evening without technology. When you awake, attune to the day, and offer you day to God with a morning offering. When you go to sleep at night, have a space of tech-free time before you get into bed so you can hear your heart.

1. Prayer Upon Waking—*I attuned to the day ahead and invited God's help*

Location_____   *I did this*___(___Minutes) No___

2. As I Lie Down to Sleep—*I offered my heart and dreams to God*

Location_____   *I did this*___(___Minutes) No___

Desolation From the Day – <u>Write no more than two sentences</u> on what decreased *your faith, your hope, and your love for God and neighbor today.*

Consolation From the Day – <u>Write no more than two sentences</u> on what increased *your faith, your hope, and your love for God and neighbor today.*

SPIRITUAL RECORD

For Weeks 1-16, try to spend twenty minutes in the morning and in the evening without technology. When you awake, attune to the day, and offer you day to God with a morning offering. When you go to sleep at night, have a space of tech-free time before you get into bed so you can hear your heart.

1. Prayer Upon Waking—*I attuned to the day ahead and invited God's help*

Location_____   *I did this*___(___Minutes) No___

2. As I Lie Down to Sleep—*I offered my heart and dreams to God*

Location_____   *I did this*___(___Minutes) No___

Desolation From the Day – <u>Write no more than two sentences</u> on what decreased *your faith, your hope, and your love for God and neighbor today.*

Consolation From the Day – <u>Write no more than two sentences</u> on what increased *your faith, your hope, and your love for God and neighbor today.*

SPIRITUAL RECORD

For Weeks 1-16, try to spend twenty minutes in the morning and in the evening without technology. When you awake, attune to the day, and offer you day to God with a morning offering. When you go to sleep at night, have a space of tech-free time before you get into bed so you can hear your heart.

1. Prayer Upon Waking—*I attuned to the day ahead and invited God's help*

Location_____   *I did this___(___Minutes)* No___

2. As I Lie Down to Sleep—*I offered my heart and dreams to God*

Location_____   *I did this___(___Minutes)* No___

Desolation From the Day – <u>Write no more than two sentences</u> **on what decreased** *your faith, your hope, and your love for God and neighbor today.*

Consolation From the Day – <u>Write no more than two sentences</u> **on what increased** *your faith, your hope, and your love for God and neighbor today.*

SPIRITUAL RECORD

For Weeks 1-16, try to spend twenty minutes in the morning and in the evening without technology. When you awake, attune to the day, and offer you day to God with a morning offering. When you go to sleep at night, have a space of tech-free time before you get into bed so you can hear your heart.

1. Prayer Upon Waking—*I attuned to the day ahead and invited God's help*

Location_____   *I did this*___(___Minutes) No___

2. As I Lie Down to Sleep—*I offered my heart and dreams to God*

Location_____   *I did this*___(___Minutes) No___

Desolation From the Day – <u>Write no more than two sentences</u> on what decreased *your faith, your hope, and your love for God and neighbor today.*

Consolation From the Day – <u>Write no more than two sentences</u> on what increased *your faith, your hope, and your love for God and neighbor today.*

SPIRITUAL RECORD

For Weeks 1-16, try to spend twenty minutes in the morning and in the evening without technology. When you awake, attune to the day, and offer you day to God with a morning offering. When you go to sleep at night, have a space of tech-free time before you get into bed so you can hear your heart.

1. Prayer Upon Waking—*I attuned to the day ahead and invited God's help*

Location_____   *I did this*___(___Minutes) No___

2. As I Lie Down to Sleep—*I offered my heart and dreams to God*

Location_____   *I did this*___(___Minutes) No___

Desolation From the Day – <u>Write no more than two sentences</u> on what decreased *your faith, your hope, and your love for God and neighbor today.*

Consolation From the Day – <u>Write no more than two sentences</u> on what increased *your faith, your hope, and your love for God and neighbor today.*

SPIRITUAL RECORD

For Weeks 1-16, try to spend twenty minutes in the morning and in the evening without technology. When you awake, attune to the day, and offer you day to God with a morning offering. When you go to sleep at night, have a space of tech-free time before you get into bed so you can hear your heart.

1. Prayer Upon Waking—*I attuned to the day ahead and invited God's help*

Location_____   *I did this*___(___Minutes) No___

2. As I Lie Down to Sleep—*I offered my heart and dreams to God*

Location_____   *I did this*___(___Minutes) No___

Desolation From the Day – Write no more than two sentences on what decreased *your faith, your hope, and your love for God and neighbor today.*

Consolation From the Day – Write no more than two sentences on what increased *your faith, your hope, and your love for God and neighbor today.*

Week 15

For Weeks 1-16, try to spend twenty minutes in the morning and in the evening without technology. When you awake, attune to the day, and offer you day to God with a morning offering. When you go to sleep at night, have a space of tech-free time before you get into bed so you can hear your heart.

1. Prayer Upon Waking—*I attuned to the day ahead and invited God's help*

Location_____ *I did this*___(___Minutes) No___

2. As I Lie Down to Sleep—*I offered my heart and dreams to God*

Location_____ *I did this*___(___Minutes) No___

Desolation From the Day – <u>Write no more than two sentences</u> on what decreased *your faith, your hope, and your love for God and neighbor today.*

Consolation From the Day – <u>Write no more than two sentences</u> on what increased *your faith, your hope, and your love for God and neighbor today.*

SPIRITUAL RECORD

For Weeks 1-16, try to spend twenty minutes in the morning and in the evening without technology. When you awake, attune to the day, and offer you day to God with a morning offering. When you go to sleep at night, have a space of tech-free time before you get into bed so you can hear your heart.

1. Prayer Upon Waking—*I attuned to the day ahead and invited God's help*

Location_____   *I did this*____(___Minutes) No___

2. As I Lie Down to Sleep—*I offered my heart and dreams to God*

Location_____   *I did this*____(___Minutes) No___

Desolation From the Day – <u>Write no more than two sentences</u> on what decreased *your faith, your hope, and your love for God and neighbor today.*

Consolation From the Day – <u>Write no more than two sentences</u> on what increased *your faith, your hope, and your love for God and neighbor today.*

SPIRITUAL RECORD

For Weeks 1-16, try to spend twenty minutes in the morning and in the evening without technology. When you awake, attune to the day, and offer you day to God with a morning offering. When you go to sleep at night, have a space of tech-free time before you get into bed so you can hear your heart.

1. Prayer Upon Waking—*I attuned to the day ahead and invited God's help*

Location_____ *I did this*___(___Minutes) No___

2. As I Lie Down to Sleep—*I offered my heart and dreams to God*

Location_____ *I did this*___(___Minutes) No___

Desolation From the Day – <u>Write no more than two sentences</u> on what decreased *your faith, your hope, and your love for God and neighbor today.*

Consolation From the Day – <u>Write no more than two sentences</u> on what increased *your faith, your hope, and your love for God and neighbor today.*

SPIRITUAL RECORD

For Weeks 1-16, try to spend twenty minutes in the morning and in the evening without technology. When you awake, attune to the day, and offer you day to God with a morning offering. When you go to sleep at night, have a space of tech-free time before you get into bed so you can hear your heart.

1. Prayer Upon Waking—*I attuned to the day ahead and invited God's help*

Location_____   *I did this___(___Minutes) No___*

2. As I Lie Down to Sleep—*I offered my heart and dreams to God*

Location_____   *I did this___(___Minutes) No___*

Desolation From the Day – <u>Write no more than two sentences</u> on what decreased *your faith, your hope, and your love for God and neighbor today.*

Consolation From the Day – <u>Write no more than two sentences</u> on what increased *your faith, your hope, and your love for God and neighbor today.*

SPIRITUAL RECORD

For Weeks 1-16, try to spend twenty minutes in the morning and in the evening without technology. When you awake, attune to the day, and offer you day to God with a morning offering. When you go to sleep at night, have a space of tech-free time before you get into bed so you can hear your heart.

1. Prayer Upon Waking—*I attuned to the day ahead and invited God's help*

Location_____   *I did this___(___Minutes) No___

2. As I Lie Down to Sleep—*I offered my heart and dreams to God*

Location_____   *I did this___(___Minutes) No___

Desolation From the Day – <u>Write no more than two sentences</u> on what decreased *your faith, your hope, and your love for God and neighbor today.*

Consolation From the Day – <u>Write no more than two sentences</u> on what increased *your faith, your hope, and your love for God and neighbor today.*

SPIRITUAL RECORD

For Weeks 1-16, try to spend twenty minutes in the morning and in the evening without technology. When you awake, attune to the day, and offer you day to God with a morning offering. When you go to sleep at night, have a space of tech-free time before you get into bed so you can hear your heart.

1. Prayer Upon Waking—*I attuned to the day ahead and invited God's help*

Location_____   *I did this*___(___Minutes) No___

2. As I Lie Down to Sleep—*I offered my heart and dreams to God*

Location_____   *I did this*___(___Minutes) No___

Desolation From the Day – <u>Write no more than two sentences</u> **on what decreased** *your faith, your hope, and your love for God and neighbor today.*

Consolation From the Day – <u>Write no more than two sentences</u> **on what increased** *your faith, your hope, and your love for God and neighbor today.*

SPIRITUAL RECORD

For Weeks 1-16, try to spend twenty minutes in the morning and in the evening without technology. When you awake, attune to the day, and offer you day to God with a morning offering. When you go to sleep at night, have a space of tech-free time before you get into bed so you can hear your heart.

1. Prayer Upon Waking—*I attuned to the day ahead and invited God's help*

Location_____   *I did this*___(___Minutes) No___

2. As I Lie Down to Sleep—*I offered my heart and dreams to God*

Location_____   *I did this*___(___Minutes) No___

Desolation From the Day – <u>Write no more than two sentences</u> on what decreased *your faith, your hope, and your love for God and neighbor today.*

Consolation From the Day – <u>Write no more than two sentences</u> on what increased *your faith, your hope, and your love for God and neighbor today.*

 # Week 16

For Weeks 1-16, try to spend twenty minutes in the morning and in the evening without technology. When you awake, attune to the day, and offer you day to God with a morning offering. When you go to sleep at night, have a space of tech-free time before you get into bed so you can hear your heart.

1. Prayer Upon Waking—*I attuned to the day ahead and invited God's help*

Location_____ *I did this*___(___Minutes) No___

2. As I Lie Down to Sleep—*I offered my heart and dreams to God*

Location_____ *I did this*___(___Minutes) No___

Desolation From the Day – <u>Write no more than two sentences</u> on what decreased *your faith, your hope, and your love for God and neighbor today.*

Consolation From the Day – <u>Write no more than two sentences</u> on what increased *your faith, your hope, and your love for God and neighbor today.*

SPIRITUAL RECORD

For Weeks 1-16, try to spend twenty minutes in the morning and in the evening without technology. When you awake, attune to the day, and offer you day to God with a morning offering. When you go to sleep at night, have a space of tech-free time before you get into bed so you can hear your heart.

1. Prayer Upon Waking—*I attuned to the day ahead and invited God's help*

Location_____   *I did this___(___Minutes) No___*

2. As I Lie Down to Sleep—*I offered my heart and dreams to God*

Location_____   *I did this___(___Minutes) No___*

Desolation From the Day – <u>Write no more than two sentences</u> on what decreased *your faith, your hope, and your love for God and neighbor today.*

Consolation From the Day – <u>Write no more than two sentences</u> on what increased *your faith, your hope, and your love for God and neighbor today.*

SPIRITUAL RECORD

For Weeks 1-16, try to spend twenty minutes in the morning and in the evening without technology. When you awake, attune to the day, and offer you day to God with a morning offering. When you go to sleep at night, have a space of tech-free time before you get into bed so you can hear your heart.

1. Prayer Upon Waking—*I attuned to the day ahead and invited God's help*

Location_____   *I did this*___(___Minutes) No___

2. As I Lie Down to Sleep—*I offered my heart and dreams to God*

Location_____   *I did this*___(___Minutes) No___

Desolation From the Day – <u>Write no more than two sentences</u> on what decreased *your faith, your hope, and your love for God and neighbor today.*

Consolation From the Day – <u>Write no more than two sentences</u> on what increased *your faith, your hope, and your love for God and neighbor today.*

SPIRITUAL RECORD

For Weeks 1-16, try to spend twenty minutes in the morning and in the evening without technology. When you awake, attune to the day, and offer you day to God with a morning offering. When you go to sleep at night, have a space of tech-free time before you get into bed so you can hear your heart.

1. Prayer Upon Waking—*I attuned to the day ahead and invited God's help*

Location_____ *I did this*___(___Minutes) No____

2. As I Lie Down to Sleep—*I offered my heart and dreams to God*

Location_____ *I did this*___(___Minutes) No____

Desolation From the Day – <u>Write no more than two sentences</u> on what decreased *your faith, your hope, and your love for God and neighbor today.*

Consolation From the Day – <u>Write no more than two sentences</u> on what increased *your faith, your hope, and your love for God and neighbor today.*

SPIRITUAL RECORD

For Weeks 1-16, try to spend twenty minutes in the morning and in the evening without technology. When you awake, attune to the day, and offer you day to God with a morning offering. When you go to sleep at night, have a space of tech-free time before you get into bed so you can hear your heart.

1. Prayer Upon Waking—*I attuned to the day ahead and invited God's help*

Location_____   *I did this*___(___Minutes) No___

2. As I Lie Down to Sleep—*I offered my heart and dreams to God*

Location_____   *I did this*___(___Minutes) No___

Desolation From the Day – <u>Write no more than two sentences</u> on what decreased *your faith, your hope, and your love for God and neighbor today.*

Consolation From the Day – <u>Write no more than two sentences</u> on what increased *your faith, your hope, and your love for God and neighbor today.*

SPIRITUAL RECORD

For Weeks 1-16, try to spend twenty minutes in the morning and in the evening without technology. When you awake, attune to the day, and offer you day to God with a morning offering. When you go to sleep at night, have a space of tech-free time before you get into bed so you can hear your heart.

1. Prayer Upon Waking—*I attuned to the day ahead and invited God's help*

Location_____   *I did this*___(___Minutes) No___

2. As I Lie Down to Sleep—*I offered my heart and dreams to God*

Location_____   *I did this*___(___Minutes) No___

Desolation From the Day – <u>Write no more than two sentences</u> on what decreased *your faith, your hope, and your love for God and neighbor today.*

Consolation From the Day – <u>Write no more than two sentences</u> on what increased *your faith, your hope, and your love for God and neighbor today.*

SPIRITUAL RECORD

For Weeks 1-16, try to spend twenty minutes in the morning and in the evening without technology. When you awake, attune to the day, and offer you day to God with a morning offering. When you go to sleep at night, have a space of tech-free time before you get into bed so you can hear your heart.

1. Prayer Upon Waking—*I attuned to the day ahead and invited God's help*

Location_____   *I did this___(___Minutes) No___*

2. As I Lie Down to Sleep—*I offered my heart and dreams to God*

Location_____   *I did this___(___Minutes) No___*

Desolation From the Day – <u>Write no more than two sentences</u> on what decreased *your faith, your hope, and your love for God and neighbor today.*

Consolation From the Day – <u>Write no more than two sentences</u> on what increased *your faith, your hope, and your love for God and neighbor today.*

 # Week 17

SPIRITUAL RECORD

1. Prayer Upon Waking—*I attuned to the day ahead and invited God's help*

Location_____ *I did this___(___Minutes)* No___

2. Exercises During the Day—*Awakening to your life*

Location_____ *I did this___(___Minutes)* No___

3. *Sacred Story* Prayer Mid-day—*Creation, Presence, Memory, Mercy, Eternity*—15 Minutes Maximum

Location_____ *I did this___(___Minutes)* No___

4. Exercises During the Day—*Awakening to your life*

Location_____ *I did this___(___Minutes)* No___

5. Prayer upon Retiring—*Attune to your heart, invite God into your dreams*

Location_____ *I did this___(___Minutes)* No___

6. Exercise Journal—1-2 Minutes Once Daily/Weekly/Monthly

Location_____ *I did this___(___Minutes)* No___

7. As I Lie Down to Sleep—1 Minute Total

Location_____ *I did this___(___Minutes)* No___

Desolation From the Day – <u>Write no more than two sentences</u> on what decreased *your faith, your hope, and your love for God and neighbor today.*

Consolation From the Day – <u>Write no more than two sentences</u> on what increased *your faith, your hope, and your love for God and neighbor today.*

SPIRITUAL RECORD

1. Prayer Upon Waking—*I attuned to the day ahead and invited God's help*

Location_____ *I did this*___(___Minutes) No___

2. Exercises During the Day—*Awakening to your life*

Location_____ *I did this*___(___Minutes) No___

3. *Sacred Story* **Prayer Mid-day—***Creation, Presence, Memory, Mercy,*   *Eternity—***15 Minutes Maximum**

Location_____ *I did this*___(___Minutes) No___

4. Exercises During the Day—*Awakening to your life*

Location_____ *I did this*___(___Minutes) No___

5. Prayer upon Retiring—*Attune to your heart, invite God into your dreams*

Location_____ *I did this*___(___Minutes) No___

6. Exercise Journal—1-2 Minutes Once Daily/Weekly/Monthly

Location_____ *I did this*___(___Minutes) No___

7. As I Lie Down to Sleep—1 Minute Total

Location_____ *I did this*___(___Minutes) No___

Desolation From the Day – <u>Write no more than two sentences</u> on what decreased *your faith, your hope, and your love for God and neighbor today.*

Consolation From the Day – <u>Write no more than two sentences</u> on what increased *your faith, your hope, and your love for God and neighbor today.*

SPIRITUAL RECORD

1. Prayer Upon Waking—*I attuned to the day ahead and invited God's help*

Location_____ *I did this*___(___Minutes) No___

2. Exercises During the Day—*Awakening to your life*

Location_____ *I did this*___(___Minutes) No___

3. *Sacred Story* **Prayer Mid-day**—*Creation, Presence, Memory, Mercy,* *Eternity*—**15 Minutes Maximum**

Location_____ *I did this*___(___Minutes) No___

4. Exercises During the Day—*Awakening to your life*

Location_____ *I did this*___(___Minutes) No___

5. Prayer upon Retiring—*Attune to your heart, invite God into your dreams*

Location_____ *I did this*___(___Minutes) No___

6. Exercise Journal—**1-2 Minutes Once Daily/Weekly/Monthly**

Location_____ *I did this*___(___Minutes) No___

7. As I Lie Down to Sleep—**1 Minute Total**

Location_____ *I did this*___(___Minutes) No___

Desolation From the Day – <u>Write no more than two sentences</u> on what decreased *your faith, your hope, and your love for God and neighbor today.*

Consolation From the Day – <u>Write no more than two sentences</u> on what increased *your faith, your hope, and your love for God and neighbor today.*

SPIRITUAL RECORD

1. Prayer Upon Waking—*I attuned to the day ahead and invited God's help*

Location_____ *I did this*___(___Minutes) No___

2. Exercises During the Day—*Awakening to your life*

Location_____ *I did this*___(___Minutes) No___

3. *Sacred Story* Prayer Mid-day—*Creation, Presence, Memory, Mercy,* *Eternity*—**15 Minutes Maximum**

Location_____ *I did this*___(___Minutes) No___

4. Exercises During the Day—*Awakening to your life*

Location_____ *I did this*___(___Minutes) No___

5. Prayer upon Retiring—*Attune to your heart, invite God into your dreams*

Location_____ *I did this*___(___Minutes) No___

6. Exercise Journal—**1-2 Minutes Once Daily/Weekly/Monthly**

Location_____ *I did this*___(___Minutes) No___

7. As I Lie Down to Sleep—**1 Minute Total**

Location_____ *I did this*___(___Minutes) No___

Desolation From the Day – <u>Write no more than two sentences</u> on what decreased *your faith, your hope, and your love for God and neighbor today.*

Consolation From the Day – <u>Write no more than two sentences</u> on what increased *your faith, your hope, and your love for God and neighbor today.*

SPIRITUAL RECORD

1. Prayer Upon Waking—*I attuned to the day ahead and invited God's help*

Location_____ *I did this___(___Minutes) No___*

2. Exercises During the Day—*Awakening to your life*

Location_____ *I did this___(___Minutes) No___*

3. *Sacred Story* Prayer Mid-day—*Creation, Presence, Memory, Mercy, Eternity*—15 Minutes Maximum

Location_____ *I did this___(___Minutes) No___*

4. Exercises During the Day—*Awakening to your life*

Location_____ *I did this___(___Minutes) No___*

5. Prayer upon Retiring—*Attune to your heart, invite God into your dreams*

Location_____ *I did this___(___Minutes) No___*

6. Exercise Journal—1-2 Minutes Once Daily/Weekly/Monthly

Location_____ *I did this___(___Minutes) No___*

7. As I Lie Down to Sleep—1 Minute Total

Location_____ *I did this___(___Minutes) No___*

Desolation From the Day – <u>Write no more than two sentences</u> on what decreased *your faith, your hope, and your love for God and neighbor today.*

Consolation From the Day – <u>Write no more than two sentences</u> on what increased *your faith, your hope, and your love for God and neighbor today.*

SPIRITUAL RECORD

1. Prayer Upon Waking—*I attuned to the day ahead and invited God's help*

Location_____   *I did this*____(____Minutes) No____

2. Exercises During the Day—*Awakening to your life*

Location_____   *I did this*____(____Minutes) No____

3. *Sacred Story* Prayer Mid-day—*Creation, Presence, Memory, Mercy,   Eternity*—15 Minutes Maximum

Location_____   *I did this*____(____Minutes) No____

4. Exercises During the Day—*Awakening to your life*

Location_____   *I did this*____(____Minutes) No____

5. Prayer upon Retiring—*Attune to your heart, invite God into your dreams*

Location_____   *I did this*____(____Minutes) No____

6. Exercise Journal—1-2 Minutes Once Daily/Weekly/Monthly

Location_____   *I did this*____(____Minutes) No____

7. As I Lie Down to Sleep—1 Minute Total

Location_____   *I did this*____(____Minutes) No____

Desolation From the Day – Write no more than two sentences on what decreased *your faith, your hope, and your love for God and neighbor today.*

Consolation From the Day – Write no more than two sentences on what increased *your faith, your hope, and your love for God and neighbor today.*

SPIRITUAL RECORD

1. Prayer Upon Waking—*I attuned to the day ahead and invited God's help*

Location_____ *I did this*___(___Minutes) No___

2. Exercises During the Day—*Awakening to your life*

Location_____ *I did this*___(___Minutes) No___

3. *Sacred Story* **Prayer Mid-day—***Creation, Presence, Memory, Mercy,   Eternity—***15 Minutes Maximum**

Location_____ *I did this*___(___Minutes) No___

4. Exercises During the Day—*Awakening to your life*

Location_____ *I did this*___(___Minutes) No___

5. Prayer upon Retiring—*Attune to your heart, invite God into your dreams*

Location_____ *I did this*___(___Minutes) No___

6. Exercise Journal—1-2 Minutes Once Daily/Weekly/Monthly

Location_____ *I did this*___(___Minutes) No___

7. As I Lie Down to Sleep—1 Minute Total

Location_____ *I did this*___(___Minutes) No___

Write the Week's Most Significant Desolation & Consolation

Desolation From the Day – <u>Write no more than two sentences</u> on what decreased *your faith, your hope, and your love for God and neighbor today.*

Consolation From the Day – <u>Write no more than two sentences</u> on what increased *your faith, your hope, and your love for God and neighbor today.*

Week 18

SPIRITUAL RECORD

1. Prayer Upon Waking—*I attuned to the day ahead and invited God's help*

Location_____ *I did this*___(___Minutes) No___

2. Exercises During the Day—*Awakening to your life*

Location_____ *I did this*___(___Minutes) No___

3. *Sacred Story* Prayer Mid-day—*Creation, Presence, Memory, Mercy,* *Eternity*—15 **Minutes Maximum**

Location_____ *I did this*___(___Minutes) No___

4. Exercises During the Day—*Awakening to your life*

Location_____ *I did this*___(___Minutes) No___

5. Prayer upon Retiring—*Attune to your heart, invite God into your dreams*

Location_____ *I did this*___(___Minutes) No___

6. Exercise Journal—1-2 Minutes Once Daily/Weekly/Monthly

Location_____ *I did this*___(___Minutes) No___

7. As I Lie Down to Sleep—1 Minute Total

Location_____ *I did this*___(___Minutes) No___

Desolation From the Day – <u>Write no more than two sentences</u> on what decreased *your faith, your hope, and your love for God and neighbor today.*

Consolation From the Day – <u>Write no more than two sentences</u> on what increased *your faith, your hope, and your love for God and neighbor today.*

SPIRITUAL RECORD

1. Prayer Upon Waking—*I attuned to the day ahead and invited God's help*

Location_____ *I did this*___(___Minutes) No___

2. Exercises During the Day—*Awakening to your life*

Location_____ *I did this*___(___Minutes) No___

3. *Sacred Story* Prayer Mid-day—*Creation, Presence, Memory, Mercy, Eternity*—15 Minutes Maximum

Location_____ *I did this*___(___Minutes) No___

4. Exercises During the Day—*Awakening to your life*

Location_____ *I did this*___(___Minutes) No___

5. Prayer upon Retiring—*Attune to your heart, invite God into your dreams*

Location_____ *I did this*___(___Minutes) No___

6. Exercise Journal—1-2 Minutes Once Daily/Weekly/Monthly

Location_____ *I did this*___(___Minutes) No___

7. As I Lie Down to Sleep—1 Minute Total

Location_____ *I did this*___(___Minutes) No___

Desolation From the Day – <u>Write no more than two sentences</u> **on what decreased *your faith, your hope, and your love for God and neighbor today.***

Consolation From the Day – <u>Write no more than two sentences</u> **on what increased *your faith, your hope, and your love for God and neighbor today.***

SPIRITUAL RECORD

1. Prayer Upon Waking—*I attuned to the day ahead and invited God's help*

Location_____ *I did this*___(___Minutes) No___

2. Exercises During the Day—*Awakening to your life*

Location_____ *I did this*___(___Minutes) No___

3. *Sacred Story* **Prayer Mid-day—***Creation, Presence, Memory, Mercy,* *Eternity—***15 Minutes Maximum**

Location_____ *I did this*___(___Minutes) No___

4. Exercises During the Day—*Awakening to your life*

Location_____ *I did this*___(___Minutes) No___

5. Prayer upon Retiring—*Attune to your heart, invite God into your dreams*

Location_____ *I did this*___(___Minutes) No___

6. Exercise Journal—1-2 Minutes Once Daily/Weekly/Monthly

Location_____ *I did this*___(___Minutes) No___

7. As I Lie Down to Sleep—1 Minute Total

Location_____ *I did this*___(___Minutes) No___

Desolation From the Day – <u>Write no more than two sentences</u> on what decreased *your faith, your hope, and your love for God and neighbor today.*

Consolation From the Day – <u>Write no more than two sentences</u> on what increased *your faith, your hope, and your love for God and neighbor today.*

SPIRITUAL RECORD

1. Prayer Upon Waking—*I attuned to the day ahead and invited God's help*

Location_____ *I did this*___(___Minutes) No___

2. Exercises During the Day—*Awakening to your life*

Location_____ *I did this*___(___Minutes) No___

3. *Sacred Story* **Prayer Mid-day—***Creation, Presence, Memory, Mercy,* *Eternity***—15 Minutes Maximum**

Location_____ *I did this*___(___Minutes) No___

4. Exercises During the Day—*Awakening to your life*

Location_____ *I did this*___(___Minutes) No___

5. Prayer upon Retiring—*Attune to your heart, invite God into your dreams*

Location_____ *I did this*___(___Minutes) No___

6. Exercise Journal—1-2 Minutes Once Daily/Weekly/Monthly

Location_____ *I did this*___(___Minutes) No___

7. As I Lie Down to Sleep—1 Minute Total

Location_____ *I did this*___(___Minutes) No___

Desolation From the Day – Write no more than two sentences **on what decreased** *your faith, your hope, and your love for God and neighbor today.*

Consolation From the Day – Write no more than two sentences **on what increased** *your faith, your hope, and your love for God and neighbor today.*

SPIRITUAL RECORD

1. Prayer Upon Waking—*I attuned to the day ahead and invited God's help*

Location_____ *I did this*___(___Minutes) No____

2. Exercises During the Day—*Awakening to your life*

Location_____ *I did this*___(___Minutes) No____

3. *Sacred Story* **Prayer Mid-day**—*Creation, Presence, Memory, Mercy,* *Eternity*—**15 Minutes Maximum**

Location_____ *I did this*___(___Minutes) No____

4. Exercises During the Day—*Awakening to your life*

Location_____ *I did this*___(___Minutes) No____

5. Prayer upon Retiring—*Attune to your heart, invite God into your dreams*

Location_____ *I did this*___(___Minutes) No____

6. Exercise Journal—**1-2 Minutes Once Daily/Weekly/Monthly**

Location_____ *I did this*___(___Minutes) No____

7. As I Lie Down to Sleep—**1 Minute Total**

Location_____ *I did this*___(___Minutes) No____

Desolation From the Day – Write no more than two sentences on what decreased *your faith, your hope, and your love for God and neighbor today.*

Consolation From the Day – Write no more than two sentences on what increased *your faith, your hope, and your love for God and neighbor today.*

SPIRITUAL RECORD

1. Prayer Upon Waking—*I attuned to the day ahead and invited God's help*

Location_____   *I did this*___(___Minutes) No___

2. Exercises During the Day—*Awakening to your life*

Location_____   *I did this*___(___Minutes) No___

3. *Sacred Story* Prayer Mid-day—*Creation, Presence, Memory, Mercy,   Eternity*—15 Minutes Maximum

Location_____   *I did this*___(___Minutes) No___

4. Exercises During the Day—*Awakening to your life*

Location_____   *I did this*___(___Minutes) No___

5. Prayer upon Retiring—*Attune to your heart, invite God into your dreams*

Location_____   *I did this*___(___Minutes) No___

6. Exercise Journal—1-2 Minutes Once Daily/Weekly/Monthly

Location_____   *I did this*___(___Minutes) No___

7. As I Lie Down to Sleep—1 Minute Total

Location_____   *I did this*___(___Minutes) No___

Desolation From the Day – <u>Write no more than two sentences</u> on what decreased *your faith, your hope, and your love for God and neighbor today.*

Consolation From the Day – <u>Write no more than two sentences</u> on what increased *your faith, your hope, and your love for God and neighbor today.*

SPIRITUAL RECORD

1. Prayer Upon Waking—*I attuned to the day ahead and invited God's help*

Location_____ *I did this*___(___Minutes) No___

2. Exercises During the Day—*Awakening to your life*

Location_____ *I did this*___(___Minutes) No___

3. *Sacred Story* **Prayer Mid-day**—*Creation, Presence, Memory, Mercy,   Eternity*—**15 Minutes Maximum**

Location_____ *I did this*___(___Minutes) No___

4. Exercises During the Day—*Awakening to your life*

Location_____ *I did this*___(___Minutes) No___

5. Prayer upon Retiring—*Attune to your heart, invite God into your dreams*

Location_____ *I did this*___(___Minutes) No___

6. Exercise Journal—**1-2 Minutes Once Daily/Weekly/Monthly**

Location_____ *I did this*___(___Minutes) No___

7. As I Lie Down to Sleep—**1 Minute Total**

Location_____ *I did this*___(___Minutes) No___

Write the Week's Most Significant Desolation & Consolation

Desolation From the Day – <u>Write no more than two sentences</u> on what decreased *your faith, your hope, and your love for God and neighbor today.*

Consolation From the Day – <u>Write no more than two sentences</u> on what increased *your faith, your hope, and your love for God and neighbor today.*

 Week 19

SPIRITUAL RECORD

1. Prayer Upon Waking—*I attuned to the day ahead and invited God's help*

Location_____ *I did this*___(___Minutes) No___

2. Exercises During the Day—*Awakening to your life*

Location_____ *I did this*___(___Minutes) No___

3. *Sacred Story* **Prayer Mid-day—***Creation, Presence, Memory, Mercy,   Eternity—***15 Minutes Maximum**

Location_____ *I did this*___(___Minutes) No___

4. Exercises During the Day—*Awakening to your life*

Location_____ *I did this*___(___Minutes) No___

5. Prayer upon Retiring—*Attune to your heart, invite God into your dreams*

Location_____ *I did this*___(___Minutes) No___

6. Exercise Journal—1-2 Minutes Once Daily/Weekly/Monthly

Location_____ *I did this*___(___Minutes) No___

7. As I Lie Down to Sleep—1 Minute Total

Location_____ *I did this*___(___Minutes) No___

Desolation From the Day – <u>Write no more than two sentences</u> on what decreased *your faith, your hope, and your love for God and neighbor today.*

Consolation From the Day – <u>Write no more than two sentences</u> on what increased *your faith, your hope, and your love for God and neighbor today.*

SPIRITUAL RECORD

1. Prayer Upon Waking—*I attuned to the day ahead and invited God's help*

Location_____ *I did this___(___Minutes) No___

2. Exercises During the Day—*Awakening to your life*

Location_____ *I did this___(___Minutes) No___

3. *Sacred Story* Prayer Mid-day—*Creation, Presence, Memory, Mercy,   Eternity*—15 Minutes Maximum

Location_____ *I did this___(___Minutes) No___

4. Exercises During the Day—*Awakening to your life*

Location_____ *I did this___(___Minutes) No___

5. Prayer upon Retiring—*Attune to your heart, invite God into your dreams*

Location_____ *I did this___(___Minutes) No___

6. Exercise Journal—1-2 Minutes Once Daily/Weekly/Monthly

Location_____ *I did this___(___Minutes) No___

7. As I Lie Down to Sleep—1 Minute Total

Location_____ *I did this___(___Minutes) No___

Desolation From the Day – <u>Write no more than two sentences</u> on what decreased *your faith, your hope, and your love for God and neighbor today.*

Consolation From the Day – <u>Write no more than two sentences</u> on what increased *your faith, your hope, and your love for God and neighbor today.*

SPIRITUAL RECORD

1. Prayer Upon Waking—*I attuned to the day ahead and invited God's help*

Location_____ *I did this*___(___Minutes) No___

2. Exercises During the Day—*Awakening to your life*

Location_____ *I did this*___(___Minutes) No___

3. *Sacred Story* Prayer Mid-day—*Creation, Presence, Memory, Mercy, Eternity*—15 Minutes Maximum

Location_____ *I did this*___(___Minutes) No___

4. Exercises During the Day—*Awakening to your life*

Location_____ *I did this*___(___Minutes) No___

5. Prayer upon Retiring—*Attune to your heart, invite God into your dreams*

Location_____ *I did this*___(___Minutes) No___

6. Exercise Journal—1-2 Minutes Once Daily/Weekly/Monthly

Location_____ *I did this*___(___Minutes) No___

7. As I Lie Down to Sleep—1 Minute Total

Location_____ *I did this*___(___Minutes) No___

Desolation From the Day – <u>Write no more than two sentences</u> on what decreased *your faith, your hope, and your love for God and neighbor today.*

Consolation From the Day – <u>Write no more than two sentences</u> on what increased *your faith, your hope, and your love for God and neighbor today.*

SPIRITUAL RECORD

1. Prayer Upon Waking—*I attuned to the day ahead and invited God's help*

Location_____ *I did this*___(___Minutes) No___

2. Exercises During the Day—*Awakening to your life*

Location_____ *I did this*___(___Minutes) No___

3. *Sacred Story* **Prayer Mid-day**—*Creation, Presence, Memory, Mercy,   Eternity*—**15 Minutes Maximum**

Location_____ *I did this*___(___Minutes) No___

4. Exercises During the Day—*Awakening to your life*

Location_____ *I did this*___(___Minutes) No___

5. Prayer upon Retiring—*Attune to your heart, invite God into your dreams*

Location_____ *I did this*___(___Minutes) No___

6. Exercise Journal—**1-2 Minutes Once Daily/Weekly/Monthly**

Location_____ *I did this*___(___Minutes) No___

7. As I Lie Down to Sleep—**1 Minute Total**

Location_____ *I did this*___(___Minutes) No___

Desolation From the Day – <u>Write no more than two sentences</u> on what decreased *your faith, your hope, and your love for God and neighbor today.*

Consolation From the Day – <u>Write no more than two sentences</u> on what increased *your faith, your hope, and your love for God and neighbor today.*

SPIRITUAL RECORD

1. Prayer Upon Waking—*I attuned to the day ahead and invited God's help*

Location_____ *I did this*___(___Minutes) No___

2. Exercises During the Day—*Awakening to your life*

Location_____ *I did this*___(___Minutes) No___

3. *Sacred Story* **Prayer Mid-day**—*Creation, Presence, Memory, Mercy,   Eternity*—**15 Minutes Maximum**

Location_____ *I did this*___(___Minutes) No___

4. Exercises During the Day—*Awakening to your life*

Location_____ *I did this*___(___Minutes) No___

5. Prayer upon Retiring—*Attune to your heart, invite God into your dreams*

Location_____ *I did this*___(___Minutes) No___

6. Exercise Journal—**1-2 Minutes Once Daily/Weekly/Monthly**

Location_____ *I did this*___(___Minutes) No___

7. As I Lie Down to Sleep—**1 Minute Total**

Location_____ *I did this*___(___Minutes) No___

Desolation From the Day – <u>Write no more than two sentences</u> on what decreased *your faith, your hope, and your love for God and neighbor today.*

Consolation From the Day – <u>Write no more than two sentences</u> on what increased *your faith, your hope, and your love for God and neighbor today.*

SPIRITUAL RECORD

1. Prayer Upon Waking—*I attuned to the day ahead and invited God's help*

Location_____ *I did this*___(___Minutes) No___

2. Exercises During the Day—*Awakening to your life*

Location_____ *I did this*___(___Minutes) No___

3. *Sacred Story* Prayer Mid-day—*Creation, Presence, Memory, Mercy,   Eternity*—15 Minutes Maximum

Location_____ *I did this*___(___Minutes) No___

4. Exercises During the Day—*Awakening to your life*

Location_____ *I did this*___(___Minutes) No___

5. Prayer upon Retiring—*Attune to your heart, invite God into your dreams*

Location_____ *I did this*___(___Minutes) No___

6. Exercise Journal—1-2 Minutes Once Daily/Weekly/Monthly

Location_____ *I did this*___(___Minutes) No___

7. As I Lie Down to Sleep—1 Minute Total

Location_____ *I did this*___(___Minutes) No___

Desolation From the Day – <u>Write no more than two sentences</u> on what decreased *your faith, your hope, and your love for God and neighbor today.*

Consolation From the Day – <u>Write no more than two sentences</u> on what increased *your faith, your hope, and your love for God and neighbor today.*

SPIRITUAL RECORD

1. Prayer Upon Waking—*I attuned to the day ahead and invited God's help*

Location_____   *I did this*___(___Minutes) No___

2. Exercises During the Day—*Awakening to your life*

Location_____   *I did this*___(___Minutes) No___

3. *Sacred Story* Prayer Mid-day—*Creation, Presence, Memory, Mercy,   Eternity*—15 Minutes Maximum

Location_____   *I did this*___(___Minutes) No___

4. Exercises During the Day—*Awakening to your life*

Location_____   *I did this*___(___Minutes) No___

5. Prayer upon Retiring—*Attune to your heart, invite God into your dreams*

Location_____   *I did this*___(___Minutes) No___

6. Exercise Journal—1-2 Minutes Once Daily/Weekly/Monthly

Location_____   *I did this*___(___Minutes) No___

7. As I Lie Down to Sleep—1 Minute Total

Location_____   *I did this*___(___Minutes) No___

Write the Week's Most Significant Desolation & Consolation

Desolation From the Day – <u>Write no more than two sentences</u> on what decreased *your faith, your hope, and your love for God and neighbor today.*

Consolation From the Day – <u>Write no more than two sentences</u> on what increased *your faith, your hope, and your love for God and neighbor today.*

 Week 20

SPIRITUAL RECORD

1. Prayer Upon Waking—*I attuned to the day ahead and invited God's help*

Location_____ *I did this*___(___Minutes) No___

2. Exercises During the Day—*Awakening to your life*

Location_____ *I did this*___(___Minutes) No___

3. *Sacred Story* **Prayer Mid-day—***Creation, Presence, Memory, Mercy,* *Eternity—***15 Minutes Maximum**

Location_____ *I did this*___(___Minutes) No___

4. Exercises During the Day—*Awakening to your life*

Location_____ *I did this*___(___Minutes) No___

5. Prayer upon Retiring—*Attune to your heart, invite God into your dreams*

Location_____ *I did this*___(___Minutes) No___

6. Exercise Journal—1-2 Minutes Once Daily/Weekly/Monthly

Location_____ *I did this*___(___Minutes) No___

7. As I Lie Down to Sleep—1 Minute Total

Location_____ *I did this*___(___Minutes) No___

Desolation From the Day – <u>Write no more than two sentences</u> on what decreased *your faith, your hope, and your love for God and neighbor today.*

Consolation From the Day – <u>Write no more than two sentences</u> on what increased *your faith, your hope, and your love for God and neighbor today.*

SPIRITUAL RECORD

1. Prayer Upon Waking—*I attuned to the day ahead and invited God's help*

Location_____ *I did this____(___Minutes) No___

2. Exercises During the Day—*Awakening to your life*

Location_____ *I did this____(___Minutes) No___

3. *Sacred Story* Prayer Mid-day—*Creation, Presence, Memory, Mercy, Eternity*—15 Minutes Maximum

Location_____ *I did this____(___Minutes) No___

4. Exercises During the Day—*Awakening to your life*

Location_____ *I did this____(___Minutes) No___

5. Prayer upon Retiring—*Attune to your heart, invite God into your dreams*

Location_____ *I did this____(___Minutes) No___

6. Exercise Journal—1-2 Minutes Once Daily/Weekly/Monthly

Location_____ *I did this____(___Minutes) No___

7. As I Lie Down to Sleep—1 Minute Total

Location_____ *I did this____(___Minutes) No___

Desolation From the Day – Write no more than two sentences on what decreased *your faith, your hope, and your love for God and neighbor today.*

Consolation From the Day – Write no more than two sentences on what increased *your faith, your hope, and your love for God and neighbor today.*

SPIRITUAL RECORD

1. Prayer Upon Waking—*I attuned to the day ahead and invited God's help*

Location_____ *I did this*___(___Minutes) No___

2. Exercises During the Day—*Awakening to your life*

Location_____ *I did this*___(___Minutes) No___

3. *Sacred Story* **Prayer Mid-day—***Creation, Presence, Memory, Mercy,   Eternity—***15 Minutes Maximum**

Location_____ *I did this*___(___Minutes) No___

4. Exercises During the Day—*Awakening to your life*

Location_____ *I did this*___(___Minutes) No___

5. Prayer upon Retiring—*Attune to your heart, invite God into your dreams*

Location_____ *I did this*___(___Minutes) No___

6. Exercise Journal—1-2 Minutes Once Daily/Weekly/Monthly

Location_____ *I did this*___(___Minutes) No___

7. As I Lie Down to Sleep—1 Minute Total

Location_____ *I did this*___(___Minutes) No___

Desolation From the Day – <u>Write no more than two sentences</u> on what decreased *your faith, your hope, and your love for God and neighbor today.*

Consolation From the Day – <u>Write no more than two sentences</u> on what increased *your faith, your hope, and your love for God and neighbor today.*

SPIRITUAL RECORD

1. Prayer Upon Waking—*I attuned to the day ahead and invited God's help*

Location_____ *I did this*___(___Minutes) No___

2. Exercises During the Day—*Awakening to your life*

Location_____ *I did this*___(___Minutes) No___

3. *Sacred Story* Prayer Mid-day—*Creation, Presence, Memory, Mercy,* *Eternity—***15 Minutes Maximum**

Location_____ *I did this*___(___Minutes) No___

4. Exercises During the Day—*Awakening to your life*

Location_____ *I did this*___(___Minutes) No___

5. Prayer upon Retiring—*Attune to your heart, invite God into your dreams*

Location_____ *I did this*___(___Minutes) No___

6. Exercise Journal—1-2 Minutes Once Daily/Weekly/Monthly

Location_____ *I did this*___(___Minutes) No___

7. As I Lie Down to Sleep—1 Minute Total

Location_____ *I did this*___(___Minutes) No___

Desolation From the Day – <u>Write no more than two sentences</u> on what decreased *your faith, your hope, and your love for God and neighbor today.*

Consolation From the Day – <u>Write no more than two sentences</u> on what increased *your faith, your hope, and your love for God and neighbor today.*

SPIRITUAL RECORD

1. Prayer Upon Waking—*I attuned to the day ahead and invited God's help*

Location_____ *I did this*___(___Minutes) No___

2. Exercises During the Day—*Awakening to your life*

Location_____ *I did this*___(___Minutes) No___

3. *Sacred Story* Prayer Mid-day—*Creation, Presence, Memory, Mercy,* *Eternity*—15 Minutes Maximum

Location_____ *I did this*___(___Minutes) No___

4. Exercises During the Day—*Awakening to your life*

Location_____ *I did this*___(___Minutes) No___

5. Prayer upon Retiring—*Attune to your heart, invite God into your dreams*

Location_____ *I did this*___(___Minutes) No___

6. Exercise Journal—1-2 Minutes Once Daily/Weekly/Monthly

Location_____ *I did this*___(___Minutes) No___

7. As I Lie Down to Sleep—1 Minute Total

Location_____ *I did this*___(___Minutes) No___

Desolation From the Day – <u>Write no more than two sentences</u> on what decreased *your faith, your hope, and your love for God and neighbor today.*

Consolation From the Day – <u>Write no more than two sentences</u> on what increased *your faith, your hope, and your love for God and neighbor today.*

SPIRITUAL RECORD

1. Prayer Upon Waking—*I attuned to the day ahead and invited God's help*

Location_____ *I did this*___(___Minutes) No___

2. Exercises During the Day—*Awakening to your life*

Location_____ *I did this*___(___Minutes) No___

3. *Sacred Story* Prayer Mid-day—*Creation, Presence, Memory, Mercy,   Eternity*—**15 Minutes Maximum**

Location_____ *I did this*___(___Minutes) No___

4. Exercises During the Day—*Awakening to your life*

Location_____ *I did this*___(___Minutes) No___

5. Prayer upon Retiring—*Attune to your heart, invite God into your dreams*

Location_____ *I did this*___(___Minutes) No___

6. Exercise Journal—**1-2 Minutes Once Daily/Weekly/Monthly**

Location_____ *I did this*___(___Minutes) No___

7. As I Lie Down to Sleep—**1 Minute Total**

Location_____ *I did this*___(___Minutes) No___

Desolation From the Day – <u>Write no more than two sentences</u> on what decreased *your faith, your hope, and your love for God and neighbor today.*

Consolation From the Day – <u>Write no more than two sentences</u> on what increased *your faith, your hope, and your love for God and neighbor today.*

SPIRITUAL RECORD

1. Prayer Upon Waking—*I attuned to the day ahead and invited God's help*

Location_____ *I did this*___(___Minutes) No___

2. Exercises During the Day—*Awakening to your life*

Location_____ *I did this*___(___Minutes) No___

3. *Sacred Story* Prayer Mid-day—*Creation, Presence, Memory, Mercy, Eternity*—**15 Minutes Maximum**

Location_____ *I did this*___(___Minutes) No___

4. Exercises During the Day—*Awakening to your life*

Location_____ *I did this*___(___Minutes) No___

5. Prayer upon Retiring—*Attune to your heart, invite God into your dreams*

Location_____ *I did this*___(___Minutes) No___

6. Exercise Journal—**1-2 Minutes Once Daily/Weekly/Monthly**

Location_____ *I did this*___(___Minutes) No___

7. As I Lie Down to Sleep—**1 Minute Total**

Location_____ *I did this*___(___Minutes) No___

Write the Month's Most Significant Desolation & Consolation

Desolation From the Day – Write no more than two sentences on what decreased *your faith, your hope, and your love for God and neighbor today.*

Consolation From the Day – Write no more than two sentences on what increased *your faith, your hope, and your love for God and neighbor today.*

 # Week 21

SPIRITUAL RECORD

1. Prayer Upon Waking—*I attuned to the day ahead and invited God's help*

Location_____ *I did this*___(___Minutes) No___

2. Exercises During the Day—*Awakening to your life*

Location_____ *I did this*___(___Minutes) No___

3. *Sacred Story* Prayer Mid-day—*Creation, Presence, Memory, Mercy, Eternity*—15 **Minutes Maximum**

Location_____ *I did this*___(___Minutes) No___

4. Exercises During the Day—*Awakening to your life*

Location_____ *I did this*___(___Minutes) No___

5. Prayer upon Retiring—*Attune to your heart, invite God into your dreams*

Location_____ *I did this*___(___Minutes) No___

6. Exercise Journal—**1-2 Minutes Once Daily/Weekly/Monthly**

Location_____ *I did this*___(___Minutes) No___

7. As I Lie Down to Sleep—**1 Minute Total**

Location_____ *I did this*___(___Minutes) No___

Desolation From the Day – <u>Write no more than two sentences</u> on what decreased *your faith, your hope, and your love for God and neighbor today.*

Consolation From the Day – <u>Write no more than two sentences</u> on what increased *your faith, your hope, and your love for God and neighbor today.*

SPIRITUAL RECORD

1. Prayer Upon Waking—*I attuned to the day ahead and invited God's help*

Location_____   *I did this*____(___Minutes) No___

2. Exercises During the Day—*Awakening to your life*

Location_____   *I did this*____(___Minutes) No___

3. *Sacred Story* **Prayer Mid-day—***Creation, Presence, Memory, Mercy,   Eternity—***15 Minutes Maximum**

Location_____   *I did this*____(___Minutes) No___

4. Exercises During the Day—*Awakening to your life*

Location_____   *I did this*____(___Minutes) No___

5. Prayer upon Retiring—*Attune to your heart, invite God into your dreams*

Location_____   *I did this*____(___Minutes) No___

6. Exercise Journal—1-2 Minutes Once Daily/Weekly/Monthly

Location_____   *I did this*____(___Minutes) No___

7. As I Lie Down to Sleep—1 Minute Total

Location_____   *I did this*____(___Minutes) No___

Desolation From the Day – Write no more than two sentences **on what decreased** *your faith, your hope, and your love for God and neighbor today.*

Consolation From the Day – Write no more than two sentences **on what increased** *your faith, your hope, and your love for God and neighbor today.*

SPIRITUAL RECORD

1. Prayer Upon Waking—*I attuned to the day ahead and invited God's help*

Location_____ *I did this*___(___Minutes) No___

2. Exercises During the Day—*Awakening to your life*

Location_____ *I did this*___(___Minutes) No___

3. *Sacred Story* Prayer Mid-day—*Creation, Presence, Memory, Mercy,   Eternity*—15 Minutes Maximum

Location_____ *I did this*___(___Minutes) No___

4. Exercises During the Day—*Awakening to your life*

Location_____ *I did this*___(___Minutes) No___

5. Prayer upon Retiring—*Attune to your heart, invite God into your dreams*

Location_____ *I did this*___(___Minutes) No___

6. Exercise Journal—1-2 Minutes Once Daily/Weekly/Monthly

Location_____ *I did this*___(___Minutes) No___

7. As I Lie Down to Sleep—1 Minute Total

Location_____ *I did this*___(___Minutes) No___

Desolation From the Day – <u>Write no more than two sentences</u> on what decreased *your faith, your hope, and your love for God and neighbor today.*

Consolation From the Day – <u>Write no more than two sentences</u> on what increased *your faith, your hope, and your love for God and neighbor today.*

SPIRITUAL RECORD

1. Prayer Upon Waking—*I attuned to the day ahead and invited God's help*

Location_____   *I did this*___(___Minutes) No___

2. Exercises During the Day—*Awakening to your life*

Location_____   *I did this*___(___Minutes) No___

3. *Sacred Story* Prayer Mid-day—*Creation, Presence, Memory, Mercy,* *Eternity*—15 Minutes Maximum

Location_____   *I did this*___(___Minutes) No___

4. Exercises During the Day—*Awakening to your life*

Location_____   *I did this*___(___Minutes) No___

5. Prayer upon Retiring—*Attune to your heart, invite God into your dreams*

Location_____   *I did this*___(___Minutes) No___

6. Exercise Journal—1-2 Minutes Once Daily/Weekly/Monthly

Location_____   *I did this*___(___Minutes) No___

7. As I Lie Down to Sleep—1 Minute Total

Location_____   *I did this*___(___Minutes) No___

Desolation From the Day – <u>Write no more than two sentences</u> on what decreased *your faith, your hope, and your love for God and neighbor today.*

Consolation From the Day – <u>Write no more than two sentences</u> on what increased *your faith, your hope, and your love for God and neighbor today.*

SPIRITUAL RECORD

1. Prayer Upon Waking—*I attuned to the day ahead and invited God's help*

Location_____ *I did this*___(___Minutes) No___

2. Exercises During the Day—*Awakening to your life*

Location_____ *I did this*___(___Minutes) No___

3. *Sacred Story* **Prayer Mid-day—***Creation, Presence, Memory, Mercy,   Eternity—***15 Minutes Maximum**

Location_____ *I did this*___(___Minutes) No___

4. Exercises During the Day—*Awakening to your life*

Location_____ *I did this*___(___Minutes) No___

5. Prayer upon Retiring—*Attune to your heart, invite God into your dreams*

Location_____ *I did this*___(___Minutes) No___

6. Exercise Journal—1-2 Minutes Once Daily/Weekly/Monthly

Location_____ *I did this*___(___Minutes) No___

7. As I Lie Down to Sleep—1 Minute Total

Location_____ *I did this*___(___Minutes) No___

Desolation From the Day – <u>Write no more than two sentences</u> on what decreased *your faith, your hope, and your love for God and neighbor today.*

Consolation From the Day – <u>Write no more than two sentences</u> on what increased *your faith, your hope, and your love for God and neighbor today.*

SPIRITUAL RECORD

1. Prayer Upon Waking—*I attuned to the day ahead and invited God's help*

Location_____   *I did this*___(___Minutes) No___

2. Exercises During the Day—*Awakening to your life*

Location_____   *I did this*___(___Minutes) No___

3. *Sacred Story* Prayer Mid-day—*Creation, Presence, Memory, Mercy,*   *Eternity*—15 Minutes Maximum

Location_____   *I did this*___(___Minutes) No___

4. Exercises During the Day—*Awakening to your life*

Location_____   *I did this*___(___Minutes) No___

5. Prayer upon Retiring—*Attune to your heart, invite God into your dreams*

Location_____   *I did this*___(___Minutes) No___

6. Exercise Journal—1-2 Minutes Once Daily/Weekly/Monthly

Location_____   *I did this*___(___Minutes) No___

7. As I Lie Down to Sleep—1 Minute Total

Location_____   *I did this*___(___Minutes) No___

Desolation From the Day – <u>Write no more than two sentences</u> on what decreased *your faith, your hope, and your love for God and neighbor today.*

Consolation From the Day – <u>Write no more than two sentences</u> on what increased *your faith, your hope, and your love for God and neighbor today.*

SPIRITUAL RECORD

1. Prayer Upon Waking—*I attuned to the day ahead and invited God's help*

Location_____ *I did this*____(____Minutes) No____

2. Exercises During the Day—*Awakening to your life*

Location_____ *I did this*____(____Minutes) No____

3. *Sacred Story* **Prayer Mid-day—***Creation, Presence, Memory, Mercy,   Eternity—***15 Minutes Maximum**

Location_____ *I did this*____(____Minutes) No____

4. Exercises During the Day—*Awakening to your life*

Location_____ *I did this*____(____Minutes) No____

5. Prayer upon Retiring—*Attune to your heart, invite God into your dreams*

Location_____ *I did this*____(____Minutes) No____

6. Exercise Journal—1-2 Minutes Once Daily/Weekly/Monthly

Location_____ *I did this*____(____Minutes) No____

7. As I Lie Down to Sleep—1 Minute Total

Location_____ *I did this*____(____Minutes) No____

Write the Week's Most Significant Desolation & Consolation

Desolation From the Day – <u>Write no more than two sentences</u> **on what decreased** *your faith, your hope, and your love for God and neighbor today.*

Consolation From the Day – <u>Write no more than two sentences</u> **on what increased** *your faith, your hope, and your love for God and neighbor today.*

Week 22

SPIRITUAL RECORD

1. Prayer Upon Waking—*I attuned to the day ahead and invited God's help*

Location_____ *I did this*___(___Minutes) No___

2. Exercises During the Day—*Awakening to your life*

Location_____ *I did this*___(___Minutes) No___

3. *Sacred Story* **Prayer Mid-day**—*Creation, Presence, Memory, Mercy,* *Eternity*—**15 Minutes Maximum**

Location_____ *I did this*___(___Minutes) No___

4. Exercises During the Day—*Awakening to your life*

Location_____ *I did this*___(___Minutes) No___

5. Prayer upon Retiring—*Attune to your heart, invite God into your dreams*

Location_____ *I did this*___(___Minutes) No___

6. Exercise Journal—**1-2 Minutes Once Daily/Weekly/Monthly**

Location_____ *I did this*___(___Minutes) No___

7. As I Lie Down to Sleep—**1 Minute Total**

Location_____ *I did this*___(___Minutes) No___

Desolation From the Day – <u>Write no more than two sentences</u> on what decreased *your faith, your hope, and your love for God and neighbor today.*

Consolation From the Day – <u>Write no more than two sentences</u> on what increased *your faith, your hope, and your love for God and neighbor today.*

SPIRITUAL RECORD

1. Prayer Upon Waking—*I attuned to the day ahead and invited God's help*

Location_____ *I did this*___(___Minutes) No___

2. Exercises During the Day—*Awakening to your life*

Location_____ *I did this*___(___Minutes) No___

3. *Sacred Story* **Prayer Mid-day—***Creation, Presence, Memory, Mercy,   Eternity—***15 Minutes Maximum**

Location_____ *I did this*___(___Minutes) No___

4. Exercises During the Day—*Awakening to your life*

Location_____ *I did this*___(___Minutes) No___

5. Prayer upon Retiring—*Attune to your heart, invite God into your dreams*

Location_____ *I did this*___(___Minutes) No___

6. Exercise Journal—1-2 Minutes Once Daily/Weekly/Monthly

Location_____ *I did this*___(___Minutes) No___

7. As I Lie Down to Sleep—1 Minute Total

Location_____ *I did this*___(___Minutes) No___

Desolation From the Day – <u>Write no more than two sentences</u> on what decreased *your faith, your hope, and your love for God and neighbor today.*

Consolation From the Day – <u>Write no more than two sentences</u> on what increased *your faith, your hope, and your love for God and neighbor today.*

SPIRITUAL RECORD

1. Prayer Upon Waking—*I attuned to the day ahead and invited God's help*

Location_____ *I did this___(___Minutes)* No___

2. Exercises During the Day—*Awakening to your life*

Location_____ *I did this___(___Minutes)* No___

3. *Sacred Story* **Prayer Mid-day—***Creation, Presence, Memory, Mercy,   Eternity—***15 Minutes Maximum**

Location_____ *I did this___(___Minutes)* No___

4. Exercises During the Day—*Awakening to your life*

Location_____ *I did this___(___Minutes)* No___

5. Prayer upon Retiring—*Attune to your heart, invite God into your dreams*

Location_____ *I did this___(___Minutes)* No___

6. Exercise Journal—1-2 Minutes Once Daily/Weekly/Monthly

Location_____ *I did this___(___Minutes)* No___

7. As I Lie Down to Sleep—1 Minute Total

Location_____ *I did this___(___Minutes)* No___

Desolation From the Day – Write no more than two sentences on what decreased *your faith, your hope, and your love for God and neighbor today.*

Consolation From the Day – Write no more than two sentences on what increased *your faith, your hope, and your love for God and neighbor today.*

SPIRITUAL RECORD

1. Prayer Upon Waking—*I attuned to the day ahead and invited God's help*

Location_____ *I did this*___(___Minutes) No___

2. Exercises During the Day—*Awakening to your life*

Location_____ *I did this*___(___Minutes) No___

3. *Sacred Story* **Prayer Mid-day—***Creation, Presence, Memory, Mercy,   Eternity*—**15 Minutes Maximum**

Location_____ *I did this*___(___Minutes) No___

4. Exercises During the Day—*Awakening to your life*

Location_____ *I did this*___(___Minutes) No___

5. Prayer upon Retiring—*Attune to your heart, invite God into your dreams*

Location_____ *I did this*___(___Minutes) No___

6. Exercise Journal—1-2 Minutes Once Daily/Weekly/Monthly

Location_____ *I did this*___(___Minutes) No___

7. As I Lie Down to Sleep—1 Minute Total

Location_____ *I did this*___(___Minutes) No___

Desolation From the Day – Write no more than two sentences on what decreased *your faith, your hope, and your love for God and neighbor today.*

Consolation From the Day – Write no more than two sentences on what increased *your faith, your hope, and your love for God and neighbor today.*

SPIRITUAL RECORD

1. Prayer Upon Waking—*I attuned to the day ahead and invited God's help*

Location_____ *I did this*___(___Minutes) No___

2. Exercises During the Day—*Awakening to your life*

Location_____ *I did this*___(___Minutes) No___

3. *Sacred Story* **Prayer Mid-day**—*Creation, Presence, Memory, Mercy,* *Eternity*—**15 Minutes Maximum**

Location_____ *I did this*___(___Minutes) No___

4. Exercises During the Day—*Awakening to your life*

Location_____ *I did this*___(___Minutes) No___

5. Prayer upon Retiring—*Attune to your heart, invite God into your dreams*

Location_____ *I did this*___(___Minutes) No___

6. Exercise Journal—**1-2 Minutes Once Daily/Weekly/Monthly**

Location_____ *I did this*___(___Minutes) No___

7. As I Lie Down to Sleep—**1 Minute Total**

Location_____ *I did this*___(___Minutes) No___

Desolation From the Day – Write no more than two sentences on what decreased *your faith, your hope, and your love for God and neighbor today.*

Consolation From the Day – Write no more than two sentences on what increased *your faith, your hope, and your love for God and neighbor today.*

SPIRITUAL RECORD

1. Prayer Upon Waking—*I attuned to the day ahead and invited God's help*

Location_____ *I did this*___(___Minutes) No___

2. Exercises During the Day—*Awakening to your life*

Location_____ *I did this*___(___Minutes) No___

3. *Sacred Story* **Prayer Mid-day**—*Creation, Presence, Memory, Mercy,   Eternity*—15 **Minutes Maximum**

Location_____ *I did this*___(___Minutes) No___

4. Exercises During the Day—*Awakening to your life*

Location_____ *I did this*___(___Minutes) No___

5. Prayer upon Retiring—*Attune to your heart, invite God into your dreams*

Location_____ *I did this*___(___Minutes) No___

6. Exercise Journal—**1-2 Minutes Once Daily/Weekly/Monthly**

Location_____ *I did this*___(___Minutes) No___

7. As I Lie Down to Sleep—**1 Minute Total**

Location_____ *I did this*___(___Minutes) No___

Desolation From the Day – <u>Write no more than two sentences</u> on what decreased *your faith, your hope, and your love for God and neighbor today.*

Consolation From the Day – <u>Write no more than two sentences</u> on what increased *your faith, your hope, and your love for God and neighbor today.*

SPIRITUAL RECORD

1. Prayer Upon Waking—*I attuned to the day ahead and invited God's help*

Location_____   *I did this*___(___Minutes) No___

2. Exercises During the Day—*Awakening to your life*

Location_____   *I did this*___(___Minutes) No___

3. *Sacred Story* **Prayer Mid-day—***Creation, Presence, Memory, Mercy,   Eternity—***15 Minutes Maximum**

Location_____   *I did this*___(___Minutes) No___

4. Exercises During the Day—*Awakening to your life*

Location_____   *I did this*___(___Minutes) No___

5. Prayer upon Retiring—*Attune to your heart, invite God into your dreams*

Location_____   *I did this*___(___Minutes) No___

6. Exercise Journal—1-2 Minutes Once Daily/Weekly/Monthly

Location_____   *I did this*___(___Minutes) No___

7. As I Lie Down to Sleep—1 Minute Total

Location_____   *I did this*___(___Minutes) No___

Write the Week's Most Significant Desolation & Consolation

Desolation From the Day – Write no more than two sentences **on what decreased** *your faith, your hope, and your love for God and neighbor today.*

Consolation From the Day – Write no more than two sentences **on what increased** *your faith, your hope, and your love for God and neighbor today.*

 Week 23

SPIRITUAL RECORD

1. Prayer Upon Waking—*I attuned to the day ahead and invited God's help*

Location_____ *I did this*___(___Minutes) No___

2. Exercises During the Day—*Awakening to your life*

Location_____ *I did this*___(___Minutes) No___

3. *Sacred Story* **Prayer Mid-day—***Creation, Presence, Memory, Mercy,   Eternity—***15 Minutes Maximum**

Location_____ *I did this*___(___Minutes) No___

4. Exercises During the Day—*Awakening to your life*

Location_____ *I did this*___(___Minutes) No___

5. Prayer upon Retiring—*Attune to your heart, invite God into your dreams*

Location_____ *I did this*___(___Minutes) No___

6. Exercise Journal—1-2 Minutes Once Daily/Weekly/Monthly

Location_____ *I did this*___(___Minutes) No___

7. As I Lie Down to Sleep—1 Minute Total

Location_____ *I did this*___(___Minutes) No___

Desolation From the Day – <u>Write no more than two sentences</u> on what decreased *your faith, your hope, and your love for God and neighbor today.*

Consolation From the Day – <u>Write no more than two sentences</u> on what increased *your faith, your hope, and your love for God and neighbor today.*

SPIRITUAL RECORD

1. Prayer Upon Waking—*I attuned to the day ahead and invited God's help*

Location_____ *I did this*___(___Minutes) No___

2. Exercises During the Day—*Awakening to your life*

Location_____ *I did this*___(___Minutes) No___

3. *Sacred Story* **Prayer Mid-day**—*Creation, Presence, Memory, Mercy,   Eternity*—**15 Minutes Maximum**

Location_____ *I did this*___(___Minutes) No___

4. Exercises During the Day—*Awakening to your life*

Location_____ *I did this*___(___Minutes) No___

5. Prayer upon Retiring—*Attune to your heart, invite God into your dreams*

Location_____ *I did this*___(___Minutes) No___

6. Exercise Journal—**1-2 Minutes Once Daily/Weekly/Monthly**

Location_____ *I did this*___(___Minutes) No___

7. As I Lie Down to Sleep—**1 Minute Total**

Location_____ *I did this*___(___Minutes) No___

Desolation From the Day – <u>Write no more than two sentences</u> on what decreased *your faith, your hope, and your love for God and neighbor today.*

Consolation From the Day – <u>Write no more than two sentences</u> on what increased *your faith, your hope, and your love for God and neighbor today.*

SPIRITUAL RECORD

1. Prayer Upon Waking—*I attuned to the day ahead and invited God's help*

Location_____   *I did this*___(___Minutes) No___

2. Exercises During the Day—*Awakening to your life*

Location_____   *I did this*___(___Minutes) No___

3. *Sacred Story* **Prayer Mid-day**—*Creation, Presence, Memory, Mercy,   Eternity*—15 **Minutes Maximum**

Location_____   *I did this*___(___Minutes) No___

4. Exercises During the Day—*Awakening to your life*

Location_____   *I did this*___(___Minutes) No___

5. Prayer upon Retiring—*Attune to your heart, invite God into your dreams*

Location_____   *I did this*___(___Minutes) No___

6. Exercise Journal—1-2 Minutes Once Daily/Weekly/Monthly

Location_____   *I did this*___(___Minutes) No___

7. As I Lie Down to Sleep—1 Minute Total

Location_____   *I did this*___(___Minutes) No___

Desolation From the Day – <u>Write no more than two sentences</u> on what decreased *your faith, your hope, and your love for God and neighbor today.*

Consolation From the Day – <u>Write no more than two sentences</u> on what increased *your faith, your hope, and your love for God and neighbor today.*

SPIRITUAL RECORD

1. Prayer Upon Waking—*I attuned to the day ahead and invited God's help*

Location_____ *I did this___*(___Minutes) No___

2. Exercises During the Day—*Awakening to your life*

Location_____ *I did this___*(___Minutes) No___

3. *Sacred Story* **Prayer Mid-day—***Creation, Presence, Memory, Mercy,   Eternity—***15 Minutes Maximum**

Location_____ *I did this___*(___Minutes) No___

4. Exercises During the Day—*Awakening to your life*

Location_____ *I did this___*(___Minutes) No___

5. Prayer upon Retiring—*Attune to your heart, invite God into your dreams*

Location_____ *I did this___*(___Minutes) No___

6. Exercise Journal—1-2 Minutes Once Daily/Weekly/Monthly

Location_____ *I did this___*(___Minutes) No___

7. As I Lie Down to Sleep—1 Minute Total

Location_____ *I did this___*(___Minutes) No___

Desolation From the Day – <u>Write no more than two sentences</u> on what decreased *your faith, your hope, and your love for God and neighbor today.*

Consolation From the Day – <u>Write no more than two sentences</u> on what increased *your faith, your hope, and your love for God and neighbor today.*

SPIRITUAL RECORD

1. Prayer Upon Waking—*I attuned to the day ahead and invited God's help*

Location_____ *I did this*___(___Minutes) No___

2. Exercises During the Day—*Awakening to your life*

Location_____ *I did this*___(___Minutes) No___

3. *Sacred Story* Prayer Mid-day—*Creation, Presence, Memory, Mercy,   Eternity*—15 Minutes Maximum

Location_____ *I did this*___(___Minutes) No___

4. Exercises During the Day—*Awakening to your life*

Location_____ *I did this*___(___Minutes) No___

5. Prayer upon Retiring—*Attune to your heart, invite God into your dreams*

Location_____ *I did this*___(___Minutes) No___

6. Exercise Journal—1-2 Minutes Once Daily/Weekly/Monthly

Location_____ *I did this*___(___Minutes) No___

7. As I Lie Down to Sleep—1 Minute Total

Location_____ *I did this*___(___Minutes) No___

Desolation From the Day – <u>Write no more than two sentences</u> on what decreased *your faith, your hope, and your love for God and neighbor today.*

Consolation From the Day – <u>Write no more than two sentences</u> on what increased *your faith, your hope, and your love for God and neighbor today.*

SPIRITUAL RECORD

1. Prayer Upon Waking—*I attuned to the day ahead and invited God's help*

Location_____ *I did this*___(___Minutes) No___

2. Exercises During the Day—*Awakening to your life*

Location_____ *I did this*___(___Minutes) No___

3. *Sacred Story* Prayer Mid-day—*Creation, Presence, Memory, Mercy,* *Eternity***—15 Minutes Maximum**

Location_____ *I did this*___(___Minutes) No___

4. Exercises During the Day—*Awakening to your life*

Location_____ *I did this*___(___Minutes) No___

5. Prayer upon Retiring—*Attune to your heart, invite God into your dreams*

Location_____ *I did this*___(___Minutes) No___

6. Exercise Journal—1-2 Minutes Once Daily/Weekly/Monthly

Location_____ *I did this*___(___Minutes) No___

7. As I Lie Down to Sleep—1 Minute Total

Location_____ *I did this*___(___Minutes) No___

Desolation From the Day – Write no more than two sentences on what decreased *your faith, your hope, and your love for God and neighbor today.*

Consolation From the Day – Write no more than two sentences on what increased *your faith, your hope, and your love for God and neighbor today.*

SPIRITUAL RECORD

1. Prayer Upon Waking—*I attuned to the day ahead and invited God's help*

Location_____ *I did this____(____Minutes) No____*

2. Exercises During the Day—*Awakening to your life*

Location_____ *I did this____(____Minutes) No____*

3. *Sacred Story* **Prayer Mid-day—***Creation, Presence, Memory, Mercy,   Eternity—*15 **Minutes Maximum**

Location_____ *I did this____(____Minutes) No____*

4. Exercises During the Day—*Awakening to your life*

Location_____ *I did this____(____Minutes) No____*

5. Prayer upon Retiring—*Attune to your heart, invite God into your dreams*

Location_____ *I did this____(____Minutes) No____*

6. Exercise Journal—1-2 Minutes Once Daily/Weekly/Monthly

Location_____ *I did this____(____Minutes) No____*

7. As I Lie Down to Sleep—1 Minute Total

Location_____ *I did this____(____Minutes) No____*

Write the Week's Most Significant Desolation & Consolation

Desolation From the Day – <u>Write no more than two sentences</u> **on what decreased** *your faith, your hope, and your love for God and neighbor today.*

Consolation From the Day – <u>Write no more than two sentences</u> **on what increased** *your faith, your hope, and your love for God and neighbor today.*

 # Week 24

SPIRITUAL RECORD

1. Prayer Upon Waking—*I attuned to the day ahead and invited God's help*

Location_____ *I did this*___(___Minutes) No___

2. Exercises During the Day—*Awakening to your life*

Location_____ *I did this*___(___Minutes) No___

3. *Sacred Story* **Prayer Mid-day**—*Creation, Presence, Memory, Mercy,   Eternity*—**15 Minutes Maximum**

Location_____ *I did this*___(___Minutes) No___

4. Exercises During the Day—*Awakening to your life*

Location_____ *I did this*___(___Minutes) No___

5. Prayer upon Retiring—*Attune to your heart, invite God into your dreams*

Location_____ *I did this*___(___Minutes) No___

6. Exercise Journal—**1-2 Minutes Once Daily/Weekly/Monthly**

Location_____ *I did this*___(___Minutes) No___

7. As I Lie Down to Sleep—**1 Minute Total**

Location_____ *I did this*___(___Minutes) No___

Desolation From the Day – <u>Write no more than two sentences</u> on what decreased *your faith, your hope, and your love for God and neighbor today.*

Consolation From the Day – <u>Write no more than two sentences</u> on what increased *your faith, your hope, and your love for God and neighbor today.*

SPIRITUAL RECORD

1. Prayer Upon Waking—*I attuned to the day ahead and invited God's help*

Location_____ *I did this*___(___Minutes) No___

2. Exercises During the Day—*Awakening to your life*

Location_____ *I did this*___(___Minutes) No___

3. *Sacred Story* Prayer Mid-day—*Creation, Presence, Memory, Mercy,   Eternity*—15 Minutes Maximum

Location_____ *I did this*___(___Minutes) No___

4. Exercises During the Day—*Awakening to your life*

Location_____ *I did this*___(___Minutes) No___

5. Prayer upon Retiring—*Attune to your heart, invite God into your dreams*

Location_____ *I did this*___(___Minutes) No___

6. Exercise Journal—1-2 Minutes Once Daily/Weekly/Monthly

Location_____ *I did this*___(___Minutes) No___

7. As I Lie Down to Sleep—1 Minute Total

Location_____ *I did this*___(___Minutes) No___

Desolation From the Day – <u>Write no more than two sentences</u> on what decreased *your faith, your hope, and your love for God and neighbor today.*

Consolation From the Day – <u>Write no more than two sentences</u> on what increased *your faith, your hope, and your love for God and neighbor today.*

SPIRITUAL RECORD

1. Prayer Upon Waking—*I attuned to the day ahead and invited God's help*

Location_____ *I did this*___(___Minutes) No____

2. Exercises During the Day—*Awakening to your life*

Location_____ *I did this*___(___Minutes) No____

3. *Sacred Story* Prayer Mid-day—*Creation, Presence, Memory, Mercy,* *Eternity***—15 Minutes Maximum**

Location_____ *I did this*___(___Minutes) No____

4. Exercises During the Day—*Awakening to your life*

Location_____ *I did this*___(___Minutes) No____

5. Prayer upon Retiring—*Attune to your heart, invite God into your dreams*

Location_____ *I did this*___(___Minutes) No____

6. Exercise Journal—1-2 Minutes Once Daily/Weekly/Monthly

Location_____ *I did this*___(___Minutes) No____

7. As I Lie Down to Sleep—1 Minute Total

Location_____ *I did this*___(___Minutes) No____

Desolation From the Day – __Write no more than two sentences__ on what decreased *your faith, your hope, and your love for God and neighbor today.*

Consolation From the Day – __Write no more than two sentences__ on what increased *your faith, your hope, and your love for God and neighbor today.*

SPIRITUAL RECORD

1. Prayer Upon Waking—*I attuned to the day ahead and invited God's help*

Location_____ *I did this*___(___Minutes) No___

2. Exercises During the Day—*Awakening to your life*

Location_____ *I did this*___(___Minutes) No___

3. *Sacred Story* **Prayer Mid-day—***Creation, Presence, Memory, Mercy,   Eternity—*15 **Minutes Maximum**

Location_____ *I did this*___(___Minutes) No___

4. Exercises During the Day—*Awakening to your life*

Location_____ *I did this*___(___Minutes) No___

5. Prayer upon Retiring—*Attune to your heart, invite God into your dreams*

Location_____ *I did this*___(___Minutes) No___

6. Exercise Journal—1-2 Minutes Once Daily/Weekly/Monthly

Location_____ *I did this*___(___Minutes) No___

7. As I Lie Down to Sleep—1 Minute Total

Location_____ *I did this*___(___Minutes) No___

Desolation From the Day – <u>Write no more than two sentences</u> on what decreased *your faith, your hope, and your love for God and neighbor today.*

Consolation From the Day – <u>Write no more than two sentences</u> on what increased *your faith, your hope, and your love for God and neighbor today.*

SPIRITUAL RECORD

1. Prayer Upon Waking—*I attuned to the day ahead and invited God's help*

Location_____ *I did this*___(___Minutes) No___

2. Exercises During the Day—*Awakening to your life*

Location_____ *I did this*___(___Minutes) No___

3. *Sacred Story* **Prayer Mid-day**—*Creation, Presence, Memory, Mercy,* *Eternity*—15 **Minutes Maximum**

Location_____ *I did this*___(___Minutes) No___

4. Exercises During the Day—*Awakening to your life*

Location_____ *I did this*___(___Minutes) No___

5. Prayer upon Retiring—*Attune to your heart, invite God into your dreams*

Location_____ *I did this*___(___Minutes) No___

6. Exercise Journal—**1-2 Minutes Once Daily/Weekly/Monthly**

Location_____ *I did this*___(___Minutes) No___

7. As I Lie Down to Sleep—**1 Minute Total**

Location_____ *I did this*___(___Minutes) No___

Desolation From the Day – <u>Write no more than two sentences</u> on what decreased *your faith, your hope, and your love for God and neighbor today.*

Consolation From the Day – <u>Write no more than two sentences</u> on what increased *your faith, your hope, and your love for God and neighbor today.*

SPIRITUAL RECORD

1. Prayer Upon Waking—*I attuned to the day ahead and invited God's help*

Location_____ *I did this*____(____Minutes) No____

2. Exercises During the Day—*Awakening to your life*

Location_____ *I did this*____(____Minutes) No____

3. *Sacred Story* **Prayer Mid-day—***Creation, Presence, Memory, Mercy,*   *Eternity—***15 Minutes Maximum**

Location_____ *I did this*____(____Minutes) No____

4. Exercises During the Day—*Awakening to your life*

Location_____ *I did this*____(____Minutes) No____

5. Prayer upon Retiring—*Attune to your heart, invite God into your dreams*

Location_____ *I did this*____(____Minutes) No____

6. Exercise Journal—1-2 Minutes Once Daily/Weekly/Monthly

Location_____ *I did this*____(____Minutes) No____

7. As I Lie Down to Sleep—1 Minute Total

Location_____ *I did this*____(____Minutes) No____

Desolation From the Day – Write no more than two sentences on what decreased *your faith, your hope, and your love for God and neighbor today.*

Consolation From the Day – Write no more than two sentences on what increased *your faith, your hope, and your love for God and neighbor today.*

SPIRITUAL RECORD

1. Prayer Upon Waking—*I attuned to the day ahead and invited God's help*

Location_____ *I did this___(___Minutes) No___*

2. Exercises During the Day—*Awakening to your life*

Location_____ *I did this___(___Minutes) No___*

3. *Sacred Story* **Prayer Mid-day—***Creation, Presence, Memory, Mercy,* *Eternity—***15 Minutes Maximum**

Location_____ *I did this___(___Minutes) No___*

4. Exercises During the Day—*Awakening to your life*

Location_____ *I did this___(___Minutes) No___*

5. Prayer upon Retiring—*Attune to your heart, invite God into your dreams*

Location_____ *I did this___(___Minutes) No___*

6. Exercise Journal—1-2 Minutes Once Daily/Weekly/Monthly

Location_____ *I did this___(___Minutes) No___*

7. As I Lie Down to Sleep—1 Minute Total

Location_____ *I did this___(___Minutes) No___*

Write the Month's Most Significant Desolation & Consolation

Desolation From the Day – Write no more than two sentences **on what decreased** *your faith, your hope, and your love for God and neighbor today.*

Consolation From the Day – Write no more than two sentences **on what increased** *your faith, your hope, and your love for God and neighbor today.*

 # Week 25

SPIRITUAL RECORD

1. Prayer Upon Waking—*I attuned to the day ahead and invited God's help*

Location_____ *I did this*___(___Minutes) No___

2. Exercises During the Day—*Awakening to your life*

Location_____ *I did this*___(___Minutes) No___

3. *Sacred Story* Prayer Mid-day—*Creation, Presence, Memory, Mercy, Eternity*—15 Minutes Maximum

Location_____ *I did this*___(___Minutes) No___

4. Exercises During the Day—*Awakening to your life*

Location_____ *I did this*___(___Minutes) No___

5. Prayer upon Retiring—*Attune to your heart, invite God into your dreams*

Location_____ *I did this*___(___Minutes) No___

6. Exercise Journal—1-2 Minutes Once Daily/Weekly/Monthly

Location_____ *I did this*___(___Minutes) No___

7. As I Lie Down to Sleep—1 Minute Total

Location_____ *I did this*___(___Minutes) No___

Desolation From the Day – <u>Write no more than two sentences</u> on what decreased *your faith, your hope, and your love for God and neighbor today.*

Consolation From the Day – <u>Write no more than two sentences</u> on what increased *your faith, your hope, and your love for God and neighbor today.*

SPIRITUAL RECORD

1. Prayer Upon Waking—*I attuned to the day ahead and invited God's help*

Location_____   *I did this*___(___Minutes) No___

2. Exercises During the Day—*Awakening to your life*

Location_____   *I did this*___(___Minutes) No___

3. *Sacred Story* **Prayer Mid-day—***Creation, Presence, Memory, Mercy,*   *Eternity***—15 Minutes Maximum**

Location_____   *I did this*___(___Minutes) No___

4. Exercises During the Day—*Awakening to your life*

Location_____   *I did this*___(___Minutes) No___

5. Prayer upon Retiring—*Attune to your heart, invite God into your dreams*

Location_____   *I did this*___(___Minutes) No___

6. Exercise Journal—1-2 Minutes Once Daily/Weekly/Monthly

Location_____   *I did this*___(___Minutes) No___

7. As I Lie Down to Sleep—1 Minute Total

Location_____   *I did this*___(___Minutes) No___

Desolation From the Day – <u>Write no more than two sentences</u> on what decreased *your faith, your hope, and your love for God and neighbor today.*

Consolation From the Day – <u>Write no more than two sentences</u> on what increased *your faith, your hope, and your love for God and neighbor today.*

SPIRITUAL RECORD

1. Prayer Upon Waking—*I attuned to the day ahead and invited God's help*

Location_____ *I did this*___(___Minutes) No___

2. Exercises During the Day—*Awakening to your life*

Location_____ *I did this*___(___Minutes) No___

3. *Sacred Story* Prayer Mid-day—*Creation, Presence, Memory, Mercy,***   ***Eternity—***15 Minutes Maximum**

Location_____ *I did this*___(___Minutes) No___

4. Exercises During the Day—*Awakening to your life*

Location_____ *I did this*___(___Minutes) No___

5. Prayer upon Retiring—*Attune to your heart, invite God into your dreams*

Location_____ *I did this*___(___Minutes) No___

6. Exercise Journal—1-2 Minutes Once Daily/Weekly/Monthly

Location_____ *I did this*___(___Minutes) No___

7. As I Lie Down to Sleep—1 Minute Total

Location_____ *I did this*___(___Minutes) No___

Desolation From the Day – <u>Write no more than two sentences</u> on what decreased *your faith, your hope, and your love for God and neighbor today.*

Consolation From the Day – <u>Write no more than two sentences</u> on what increased *your faith, your hope, and your love for God and neighbor today.*

SPIRITUAL RECORD

1. Prayer Upon Waking—*I attuned to the day ahead and invited God's help*

Location_____ *I did this*___(___Minutes) No___

2. Exercises During the Day—*Awakening to your life*

Location_____ *I did this*___(___Minutes) No___

3. *Sacred Story* Prayer Mid-day—*Creation, Presence, Memory, Mercy, Eternity*—15 **Minutes Maximum**

Location_____ *I did this*___(___Minutes) No___

4. Exercises During the Day—*Awakening to your life*

Location_____ *I did this*___(___Minutes) No___

5. Prayer upon Retiring—*Attune to your heart, invite God into your dreams*

Location_____ *I did this*___(___Minutes) No___

6. Exercise Journal—1-2 Minutes Once Daily/Weekly/Monthly

Location_____ *I did this*___(___Minutes) No___

7. As I Lie Down to Sleep—1 Minute Total

Location_____ *I did this*___(___Minutes) No___

Desolation From the Day – <u>Write no more than two sentences</u> on what decreased *your faith, your hope, and your love for God and neighbor today.*

Consolation From the Day – <u>Write no more than two sentences</u> on what increased *your faith, your hope, and your love for God and neighbor today.*

SPIRITUAL RECORD

1. Prayer Upon Waking—*I attuned to the day ahead and invited God's help*

Location_____ *I did this*___(___Minutes) No___

2. Exercises During the Day—*Awakening to your life*

Location_____ *I did this*___(___Minutes) No___

3. *Sacred Story* Prayer Mid-day—*Creation, Presence, Memory, Mercy, Eternity*—15 Minutes Maximum

Location_____ *I did this*___(___Minutes) No___

4. Exercises During the Day—*Awakening to your life*

Location_____ *I did this*___(___Minutes) No___

5. Prayer upon Retiring—*Attune to your heart, invite God into your dreams*

Location_____ *I did this*___(___Minutes) No___

6. Exercise Journal—1-2 Minutes Once Daily/Weekly/Monthly

Location_____ *I did this*___(___Minutes) No___

7. As I Lie Down to Sleep—1 Minute Total

Location_____ *I did this*___(___Minutes) No___

Desolation From the Day – <u>Write no more than two sentences</u> on what decreased *your faith, your hope, and your love for God and neighbor today.*

Consolation From the Day – <u>Write no more than two sentences</u> on what increased *your faith, your hope, and your love for God and neighbor today.*

SPIRITUAL RECORD

1. Prayer Upon Waking—*I attuned to the day ahead and invited God's help*

Location_____   *I did this*___(___Minutes) No___

2. Exercises During the Day—*Awakening to your life*

Location_____   *I did this*___(___Minutes) No___

3. *Sacred Story* **Prayer Mid-day**—*Creation, Presence, Memory, Mercy,   Eternity*—15 **Minutes Maximum**

Location_____   *I did this*___(___Minutes) No___

4. Exercises During the Day—*Awakening to your life*

Location_____   *I did this*___(___Minutes) No___

5. Prayer upon Retiring—*Attune to your heart, invite God into your dreams*

Location_____   *I did this*___(___Minutes) No___

6. Exercise Journal—**1-2 Minutes Once Daily/Weekly/Monthly**

Location_____   *I did this*___(___Minutes) No___

7. As I Lie Down to Sleep—**1 Minute Total**

Location_____   *I did this*___(___Minutes) No___

Desolation From the Day – <u>Write no more than two sentences</u> on what decreased *your faith, your hope, and your love for God and neighbor today.*

Consolation From the Day – <u>Write no more than two sentences</u> on what increased *your faith, your hope, and your love for God and neighbor today.*

SPIRITUAL RECORD

1. Prayer Upon Waking—*I attuned to the day ahead and invited God's help*

Location_____ *I did this*___(___Minutes) No___

2. Exercises During the Day—*Awakening to your life*

Location_____ *I did this*___(___Minutes) No___

3. *Sacred Story* Prayer Mid-day—*Creation, Presence, Memory, Mercy,* *Eternity*—15 **Minutes Maximum**

Location_____ *I did this*___(___Minutes) No___

4. Exercises During the Day—*Awakening to your life*

Location_____ *I did this*___(___Minutes) No___

5. Prayer upon Retiring—*Attune to your heart, invite God into your dreams*

Location_____ *I did this*___(___Minutes) No___

6. Exercise Journal—1-2 Minutes Once Daily/Weekly/Monthly

Location_____ *I did this*___(___Minutes) No___

7. As I Lie Down to Sleep—1 Minute Total

Location_____ *I did this*___(___Minutes) No___

Desolation From the Day – <u>Write no more than two sentences</u> on what decreased *your faith, your hope, and your love for God and neighbor today.*

Consolation From the Day – <u>Write no more than two sentences</u> on what increased *your faith, your hope, and your love for God and neighbor today.*

SPIRITUAL RECORD

1. Prayer Upon Waking—*I attuned to the day ahead and invited God's help*

Location_____ *I did this*___(___Minutes) No___

2. Exercises During the Day—*Awakening to your life*

Location_____ *I did this*___(___Minutes) No___

3. *Sacred Story* Prayer Mid-day—*Creation, Presence, Memory, Mercy,*   *Eternity*—15 Minutes Maximum

Location_____ *I did this*___(___Minutes) No___

4. Exercises During the Day—*Awakening to your life*

Location_____ *I did this*___(___Minutes) No___

5. Prayer upon Retiring—*Attune to your heart, invite God into your dreams*

Location_____ *I did this*___(___Minutes) No___

6. Exercise Journal—1-2 Minutes Once Daily/Weekly/Monthly

Location_____ *I did this*___(___Minutes) No___

7. As I Lie Down to Sleep—1 Minute Total

Location_____ *I did this*___(___Minutes) No___

Write the Week's Most Significant Desolation & Consolation

Desolation From the Day – <u>Write no more than two sentences</u> on what decreased *your faith, your hope, and your love for God and neighbor today.*

Consolation From the Day – <u>Write no more than two sentences</u> on what increased *your faith, your hope, and your love for God and neighbor today.*

 # Week 26

SPIRITUAL RECORD

1. Prayer Upon Waking—*I attuned to the day ahead and invited God's help*

Location_____ *I did this*___(___Minutes) No___

2. Exercises During the Day—*Awakening to your life*

Location_____ *I did this*___(___Minutes) No___

3. *Sacred Story* **Prayer Mid-day**—*Creation, Presence, Memory, Mercy,   Eternity*—**15 Minutes Maximum**

Location_____ *I did this*___(___Minutes) No___

4. Exercises During the Day—*Awakening to your life*

Location_____ *I did this*___(___Minutes) No___

5. Prayer upon Retiring—*Attune to your heart, invite God into your dreams*

Location_____ *I did this*___(___Minutes) No___

6. Exercise Journal—**1-2 Minutes Once Daily/Weekly/Monthly**

Location_____ *I did this*___(___Minutes) No___

7. As I Lie Down to Sleep—**1 Minute Total**

Location_____ *I did this*___(___Minutes) No___

Desolation From the Day – <u>Write no more than two sentences</u> on what decreased *your faith, your hope, and your love for God and neighbor today.*

Consolation From the Day – <u>Write no more than two sentences</u> on what increased *your faith, your hope, and your love for God and neighbor today.*

SPIRITUAL RECORD

1. Prayer Upon Waking—*I attuned to the day ahead and invited God's help*

Location_____ *I did this*___(___Minutes) No___

2. Exercises During the Day—*Awakening to your life*

Location_____ *I did this*___(___Minutes) No___

3. *Sacred Story* Prayer Mid-day—*Creation, Presence, Memory, Mercy,   Eternity—***15 Minutes Maximum**

Location_____ *I did this*___(___Minutes) No___

4. Exercises During the Day—*Awakening to your life*

Location_____ *I did this*___(___Minutes) No___

5. Prayer upon Retiring—*Attune to your heart, invite God into your dreams*

Location_____ *I did this*___(___Minutes) No___

6. Exercise Journal—1-2 Minutes Once Daily/Weekly/Monthly

Location_____ *I did this*___(___Minutes) No___

7. As I Lie Down to Sleep—1 Minute Total

Location_____ *I did this*___(___Minutes) No___

Desolation From the Day – <u>Write no more than two sentences</u> on what decreased *your faith, your hope, and your love for God and neighbor today.*

Consolation From the Day – <u>Write no more than two sentences</u> on what increased *your faith, your hope, and your love for God and neighbor today.*

SPIRITUAL RECORD

1. Prayer Upon Waking—*I attuned to the day ahead and invited God's help*

Location_____ *I did this*___(___Minutes) No___

2. Exercises During the Day—*Awakening to your life*

Location_____ *I did this*___(___Minutes) No___

3. *Sacred Story* **Prayer Mid-day—***Creation, Presence, Memory, Mercy,   Eternity—***15 Minutes Maximum**

Location_____ *I did this*___(___Minutes) No___

4. Exercises During the Day—*Awakening to your life*

Location_____ *I did this*___(___Minutes) No___

5. Prayer upon Retiring—*Attune to your heart, invite God into your dreams*

Location_____ *I did this*___(___Minutes) No___

6. Exercise Journal—1-2 Minutes Once Daily/Weekly/Monthly

Location_____ *I did this*___(___Minutes) No___

7. As I Lie Down to Sleep—1 Minute Total

Location_____ *I did this*___(___Minutes) No___

Desolation From the Day – <u>Write no more than two sentences</u> on what decreased *your faith, your hope, and your love for God and neighbor today.*

Consolation From the Day – <u>Write no more than two sentences</u> on what increased *your faith, your hope, and your love for God and neighbor today.*

SPIRITUAL RECORD

1. Prayer Upon Waking—*I attuned to the day ahead and invited God's help*

Location_____ *I did this*___(___Minutes) No___

2. Exercises During the Day—*Awakening to your life*

Location_____ *I did this*___(___Minutes) No___

3. *Sacred Story* **Prayer Mid-day—***Creation, Presence, Memory, Mercy,* *Eternity—***15 Minutes Maximum**

Location_____ *I did this*___(___Minutes) No___

4. Exercises During the Day—*Awakening to your life*

Location_____ *I did this*___(___Minutes) No___

5. Prayer upon Retiring—*Attune to your heart, invite God into your dreams*

Location_____ *I did this*___(___Minutes) No___

6. Exercise Journal—1-2 Minutes Once Daily/Weekly/Monthly

Location_____ *I did this*___(___Minutes) No___

7. As I Lie Down to Sleep—1 Minute Total

Location_____ *I did this*___(___Minutes) No___

Desolation From the Day – <u>Write no more than two sentences</u> on what decreased *your faith, your hope, and your love for God and neighbor today.*

Consolation From the Day – <u>Write no more than two sentences</u> on what increased *your faith, your hope, and your love for God and neighbor today.*

SPIRITUAL RECORD

1. Prayer Upon Waking—*I attuned to the day ahead and invited God's help*

Location_____ *I did this*___(___Minutes) No___

2. Exercises During the Day—*Awakening to your life*

Location_____ *I did this*___(___Minutes) No___

3. *Sacred Story* Prayer Mid-day—*Creation, Presence, Memory, Mercy,   Eternity*—15 Minutes Maximum

Location_____ *I did this*___(___Minutes) No___

4. Exercises During the Day—*Awakening to your life*

Location_____ *I did this*___(___Minutes) No___

5. Prayer upon Retiring—*Attune to your heart, invite God into your dreams*

Location_____ *I did this*___(___Minutes) No___

6. Exercise Journal—1-2 Minutes Once Daily/Weekly/Monthly

Location_____ *I did this*___(___Minutes) No___

7. As I Lie Down to Sleep—1 Minute Total

Location_____ *I did this*___(___Minutes) No___

Desolation From the Day – <u>Write no more than two sentences</u> on what decreased *your faith, your hope, and your love for God and neighbor today.*

Consolation From the Day – <u>Write no more than two sentences</u> on what increased *your faith, your hope, and your love for God and neighbor today.*

SPIRITUAL RECORD

1. Prayer Upon Waking—*I attuned to the day ahead and invited God's help*

Location_____ *I did this*___(___Minutes) No___

2. Exercises During the Day—*Awakening to your life*

Location_____ *I did this*___(___Minutes) No___

3. *Sacred Story* Prayer Mid-day—*Creation, Presence, Memory, Mercy,* *Eternity*—15 **Minutes Maximum**

Location_____ *I did this*___(___Minutes) No___

4. Exercises During the Day—*Awakening to your life*

Location_____ *I did this*___(___Minutes) No___

5. Prayer upon Retiring—*Attune to your heart, invite God into your dreams*

Location_____ *I did this*___(___Minutes) No___

6. Exercise Journal—**1-2 Minutes Once Daily/Weekly/Monthly**

Location_____ *I did this*___(___Minutes) No___

7. As I Lie Down to Sleep—**1 Minute Total**

Location_____ *I did this*___(___Minutes) No___

Desolation From the Day – Write no more than two sentences on what decreased *your faith, your hope, and your love for God and neighbor today.*

Consolation From the Day – Write no more than two sentences on what increased *your faith, your hope, and your love for God and neighbor today.*

SPIRITUAL RECORD

1. Prayer Upon Waking—*I attuned to the day ahead and invited God's help*

Location_____ *I did this*___(___Minutes) No___

2. Exercises During the Day—*Awakening to your life*

Location_____ *I did this*___(___Minutes) No___

3. *Sacred Story* Prayer Mid-day—*Creation, Presence, Memory, Mercy,   Eternity*—15 Minutes Maximum

Location_____ *I did this*___(___Minutes) No___

4. Exercises During the Day—*Awakening to your life*

Location_____ *I did this*___(___Minutes) No___

5. Prayer upon Retiring—*Attune to your heart, invite God into your dreams*

Location_____ *I did this*___(___Minutes) No___

6. Exercise Journal—1-2 Minutes Once Daily/Weekly/Monthly

Location_____ *I did this*___(___Minutes) No___

7. As I Lie Down to Sleep—1 Minute Total

Location_____ *I did this*___(___Minutes) No___

Write the Week's Most Significant Desolation & Consolation

Desolation From the Day – <u>Write no more than two sentences</u> on what decreased *your faith, your hope, and your love for God and neighbor today.*

Consolation From the Day – <u>Write no more than two sentences</u> on what increased *your faith, your hope, and your love for God and neighbor today.*

Week 27

SPIRITUAL RECORD

1. Prayer Upon Waking—*I attuned to the day ahead and invited God's help*

Location_____ *I did this*___(___Minutes) No___

2. Exercises During the Day—*Awakening to your life*

Location_____ *I did this*___(___Minutes) No___

3. *Sacred Story* Prayer Mid-day—*Creation, Presence, Memory, Mercy, Eternity*—15 Minutes Maximum

Location_____ *I did this*___(___Minutes) No___

4. Exercises During the Day—*Awakening to your life*

Location_____ *I did this*___(___Minutes) No___

5. Prayer upon Retiring—*Attune to your heart, invite God into your dreams*

Location_____ *I did this*___(___Minutes) No___

6. Exercise Journal—1-2 Minutes Once Daily/Weekly/Monthly

Location_____ *I did this*___(___Minutes) No___

7. As I Lie Down to Sleep—1 Minute Total

Location_____ *I did this*___(___Minutes) No___

Desolation From the Day – <u>Write no more than two sentences</u> on what decreased *your faith, your hope, and your love for God and neighbor today.*

Consolation From the Day – <u>Write no more than two sentences</u> on what increased *your faith, your hope, and your love for God and neighbor today.*

187

SPIRITUAL RECORD

1. Prayer Upon Waking—*I attuned to the day ahead and invited God's help*

Location_____ *I did this*___(___Minutes) No___

2. Exercises During the Day—*Awakening to your life*

Location_____ *I did this*___(___Minutes) No___

3. *Sacred Story* **Prayer Mid-day—***Creation, Presence, Memory, Mercy,   Eternity—***15 Minutes Maximum**

Location_____ *I did this*___(___Minutes) No___

4. Exercises During the Day—*Awakening to your life*

Location_____ *I did this*___(___Minutes) No___

5. Prayer upon Retiring—*Attune to your heart, invite God into your dreams*

Location_____ *I did this*___(___Minutes) No___

6. Exercise Journal—1-2 Minutes Once Daily/Weekly/Monthly

Location_____ *I did this*___(___Minutes) No___

7. As I Lie Down to Sleep—1 Minute Total

Location_____ *I did this*___(___Minutes) No___

Desolation From the Day – Write no more than two sentences on what decreased *your faith, your hope, and your love for God and neighbor today.*

Consolation From the Day – Write no more than two sentences on what increased *your faith, your hope, and your love for God and neighbor today.*

SPIRITUAL RECORD

1. Prayer Upon Waking—*I attuned to the day ahead and invited God's help*

Location_____ *I did this*____(____Minutes) No____

2. Exercises During the Day—*Awakening to your life*

Location_____ *I did this*____(____Minutes) No____

3. *Sacred Story* Prayer Mid-day—*Creation, Presence, Memory, Mercy,* *Eternity*—**15 Minutes Maximum**

Location_____ *I did this*____(____Minutes) No____

4. Exercises During the Day—*Awakening to your life*

Location_____ *I did this*____(____Minutes) No____

5. Prayer upon Retiring—*Attune to your heart, invite God into your dreams*

Location_____ *I did this*____(____Minutes) No____

6. Exercise Journal—1-2 Minutes Once Daily/Weekly/Monthly

Location_____ *I did this*____(____Minutes) No____

7. As I Lie Down to Sleep—1 Minute Total

Location_____ *I did this*____(____Minutes) No____

Desolation From the Day – Write no more than two sentences **on what decreased** *your faith, your hope, and your love for God and neighbor today.*

Consolation From the Day – Write no more than two sentences **on what increased** *your faith, your hope, and your love for God and neighbor today.*

SPIRITUAL RECORD

1. Prayer Upon Waking—*I attuned to the day ahead and invited God's help*

Location_____ *I did this*___(___Minutes) No___

2. Exercises During the Day—*Awakening to your life*

Location_____ *I did this*___(___Minutes) No___

3. *Sacred Story* **Prayer Mid-day**—*Creation, Presence, Memory, Mercy,   Eternity*—15 **Minutes Maximum**

Location_____ *I did this*___(___Minutes) No___

4. Exercises During the Day—*Awakening to your life*

Location_____ *I did this*___(___Minutes) No___

5. Prayer upon Retiring—*Attune to your heart, invite God into your dreams*

Location_____ *I did this*___(___Minutes) No___

6. Exercise Journal—**1-2 Minutes Once Daily/Weekly/Monthly**

Location_____ *I did this*___(___Minutes) No___

7. As I Lie Down to Sleep—**1 Minute Total**

Location_____ *I did this*___(___Minutes) No___

Desolation From the Day – Write no more than two sentences on what decreased *your faith, your hope, and your love for God and neighbor today.*

Consolation From the Day – Write no more than two sentences on what increased *your faith, your hope, and your love for God and neighbor today.*

SPIRITUAL RECORD

1. Prayer Upon Waking—*I attuned to the day ahead and invited God's help*

Location_____ *I did this*___(___Minutes) No___

2. Exercises During the Day—*Awakening to your life*

Location_____ *I did this*___(___Minutes) No___

3. *Sacred Story* Prayer Mid-day—*Creation, Presence, Memory, Mercy,* *Eternity*—**15 Minutes Maximum**

Location_____ *I did this*___(___Minutes) No___

4. Exercises During the Day—*Awakening to your life*

Location_____ *I did this*___(___Minutes) No___

5. Prayer upon Retiring—*Attune to your heart, invite God into your dreams*

Location_____ *I did this*___(___Minutes) No___

6. Exercise Journal—1-2 Minutes Once Daily/Weekly/Monthly

Location_____ *I did this*___(___Minutes) No___

7. As I Lie Down to Sleep—1 Minute Total

Location_____ *I did this*___(___Minutes) No___

Desolation From the Day – <u>Write no more than two sentences</u> on what decreased *your faith, your hope, and your love for God and neighbor today.*

Consolation From the Day – <u>Write no more than two sentences</u> on what increased *your faith, your hope, and your love for God and neighbor today.*

SPIRITUAL RECORD

1. Prayer Upon Waking—*I attuned to the day ahead and invited God's help*

Location_____ *I did this*___(___Minutes) No___

2. Exercises During the Day—*Awakening to your life*

Location_____ *I did this*___(___Minutes) No___

3. *Sacred Story* Prayer Mid-day—*Creation, Presence, Memory, Mercy,   Eternity*—15 Minutes Maximum

Location_____ *I did this*___(___Minutes) No___

4. Exercises During the Day—*Awakening to your life*

Location_____ *I did this*___(___Minutes) No___

5. Prayer upon Retiring—*Attune to your heart, invite God into your dreams*

Location_____ *I did this*___(___Minutes) No___

6. Exercise Journal—1-2 Minutes Once Daily/Weekly/Monthly

Location_____ *I did this*___(___Minutes) No___

7. As I Lie Down to Sleep—1 Minute Total

Location_____ *I did this*___(___Minutes) No___

Desolation From the Day – <u>Write no more than two sentences</u> on what decreased *your faith, your hope, and your love for God and neighbor today.*

Consolation From the Day – <u>Write no more than two sentences</u> on what increased *your faith, your hope, and your love for God and neighbor today.*

SPIRITUAL RECORD

1. Prayer Upon Waking—*I attuned to the day ahead and invited God's help*

Location_____   *I did this*___(___Minutes) No___

2. Exercises During the Day—*Awakening to your life*

Location_____   *I did this*___(___Minutes) No___

3. *Sacred Story* **Prayer Mid-day—***Creation, Presence, Memory, Mercy,   Eternity—***15 Minutes Maximum**

Location_____   *I did this*___(___Minutes) No___

4. Exercises During the Day—*Awakening to your life*

Location_____   *I did this*___(___Minutes) No___

5. Prayer upon Retiring—*Attune to your heart, invite God into your dreams*

Location_____   *I did this*___(___Minutes) No___

6. Exercise Journal—1-2 Minutes Once Daily/Weekly/Monthly

Location_____   *I did this*___(___Minutes) No___

7. As I Lie Down to Sleep—1 Minute Total

Location_____   *I did this*___(___Minutes) No___

Write the Week's Most Significant Desolation & Consolation

Desolation From the Day – <u>Write no more than two sentences</u> on what decreased *your faith, your hope, and your love for God and neighbor today.*

Consolation From the Day – <u>Write no more than two sentences</u> on what increased *your faith, your hope, and your love for God and neighbor today.*

 # Week 28

SPIRITUAL RECORD

1. Prayer Upon Waking—*I attuned to the day ahead and invited God's help*

Location_____ *I did this*___(___Minutes) No___

2. Exercises During the Day—*Awakening to your life*

Location_____ *I did this*___(___Minutes) No___

3. *Sacred Story* Prayer Mid-day—*Creation, Presence, Memory, Mercy, Eternity—***15 Minutes Maximum**

Location_____ *I did this*___(___Minutes) No___

4. Exercises During the Day—*Awakening to your life*

Location_____ *I did this*___(___Minutes) No___

5. Prayer upon Retiring—*Attune to your heart, invite God into your dreams*

Location_____ *I did this*___(___Minutes) No___

6. Exercise Journal—1-2 Minutes Once Daily/Weekly/Monthly

Location_____ *I did this*___(___Minutes) No___

7. As I Lie Down to Sleep—1 Minute Total

Location_____ *I did this*___(___Minutes) No___

Desolation From the Day – <u>Write no more than two sentences</u> on what decreased *your faith, your hope, and your love for God and neighbor today.*

Consolation From the Day – <u>Write no more than two sentences</u> on what increased *your faith, your hope, and your love for God and neighbor today.*

SPIRITUAL RECORD

1. Prayer Upon Waking—*I attuned to the day ahead and invited God's help*

Location_____ *I did this*____(____Minutes) No____

2. Exercises During the Day—*Awakening to your life*

Location_____ *I did this*____(____Minutes) No____

3. *Sacred Story* Prayer Mid-day—*Creation, Presence, Memory, Mercy,* *Eternity*—**15 Minutes Maximum**

Location_____ *I did this*____(____Minutes) No____

4. Exercises During the Day—*Awakening to your life*

Location_____ *I did this*____(____Minutes) No____

5. Prayer upon Retiring—*Attune to your heart, invite God into your dreams*

Location_____ *I did this*____(____Minutes) No____

6. Exercise Journal—1-2 Minutes Once Daily/Weekly/Monthly

Location_____ *I did this*____(____Minutes) No____

7. As I Lie Down to Sleep—1 Minute Total

Location_____ *I did this*____(____Minutes) No____

Desolation From the Day – Write no more than two sentences **on what decreased** *your faith, your hope, and your love for God and neighbor today.*

Consolation From the Day – Write no more than two sentences **on what increased** *your faith, your hope, and your love for God and neighbor today.*

SPIRITUAL RECORD

1. Prayer Upon Waking—*I attuned to the day ahead and invited God's help*

Location_____ *I did this*___(___Minutes) No___

2. Exercises During the Day—*Awakening to your life*

Location_____ *I did this*___(___Minutes) No___

3. *Sacred Story* Prayer Mid-day—*Creation, Presence, Memory, Mercy, Eternity*—15 Minutes Maximum

Location_____ *I did this*___(___Minutes) No___

4. Exercises During the Day—*Awakening to your life*

Location_____ *I did this*___(___Minutes) No___

5. Prayer upon Retiring—*Attune to your heart, invite God into your dreams*

Location_____ *I did this*___(___Minutes) No___

6. Exercise Journal—1-2 Minutes Once Daily/Weekly/Monthly

Location_____ *I did this*___(___Minutes) No___

7. As I Lie Down to Sleep—1 Minute Total

Location_____ *I did this*___(___Minutes) No___

Desolation From the Day – <u>Write no more than two sentences</u> on what decreased *your faith, your hope, and your love for God and neighbor today.*

Consolation From the Day – <u>Write no more than two sentences</u> on what increased *your faith, your hope, and your love for God and neighbor today.*

SPIRITUAL RECORD

1. Prayer Upon Waking—*I attuned to the day ahead and invited God's help*

Location_____ *I did this*___(___Minutes) No___

2. Exercises During the Day—*Awakening to your life*

Location_____ *I did this*___(___Minutes) No___

3. *Sacred Story* **Prayer Mid-day—***Creation, Presence, Memory, Mercy,* *Eternity—*15 **Minutes Maximum**

Location_____ *I did this*___(___Minutes) No___

4. Exercises During the Day—*Awakening to your life*

Location_____ *I did this*___(___Minutes) No___

5. Prayer upon Retiring—*Attune to your heart, invite God into your dreams*

Location_____ *I did this*___(___Minutes) No___

6. Exercise Journal—1-2 Minutes Once Daily/Weekly/Monthly

Location_____ *I did this*___(___Minutes) No___

7. As I Lie Down to Sleep—1 Minute Total

Location_____ *I did this*___(___Minutes) No___

Desolation From the Day – <u>Write no more than two sentences</u> on what decreased *your faith, your hope, and your love for God and neighbor today.*

Consolation From the Day – <u>Write no more than two sentences</u> on what increased *your faith, your hope, and your love for God and neighbor today.*

SPIRITUAL RECORD

1. Prayer Upon Waking—*I attuned to the day ahead and invited God's help*

Location_____ *I did this*___(___Minutes) No___

2. Exercises During the Day—*Awakening to your life*

Location_____ *I did this*___(___Minutes) No___

3. *Sacred Story* **Prayer Mid-day—***Creation, Presence, Memory, Mercy,   Eternity—***15 Minutes Maximum**

Location_____ *I did this*___(___Minutes) No___

4. Exercises During the Day—*Awakening to your life*

Location_____ *I did this*___(___Minutes) No___

5. Prayer upon Retiring—*Attune to your heart, invite God into your dreams*

Location_____ *I did this*___(___Minutes) No___

6. Exercise Journal—1-2 Minutes Once Daily/Weekly/Monthly

Location_____ *I did this*___(___Minutes) No___

7. As I Lie Down to Sleep—1 Minute Total

Location_____ *I did this*___(___Minutes) No___

Desolation From the Day – <u>Write no more than two sentences</u> on what decreased *your faith, your hope, and your love for God and neighbor today.*

Consolation From the Day – <u>Write no more than two sentences</u> on what increased *your faith, your hope, and your love for God and neighbor today.*

SPIRITUAL RECORD

1. Prayer Upon Waking—*I attuned to the day ahead and invited God's help*

Location_____ *I did this*___(___Minutes) No___

2. Exercises During the Day—*Awakening to your life*

Location_____ *I did this*___(___Minutes) No___

3. *Sacred Story* Prayer Mid-day—*Creation, Presence, Memory, Mercy,*   *Eternity***—15 Minutes Maximum**

Location_____ *I did this*___(___Minutes) No___

4. Exercises During the Day—*Awakening to your life*

Location_____ *I did this*___(___Minutes) No___

5. Prayer upon Retiring—*Attune to your heart, invite God into your dreams*

Location_____ *I did this*___(___Minutes) No___

6. Exercise Journal—1-2 Minutes Once Daily/Weekly/Monthly

Location_____ *I did this*___(___Minutes) No___

7. As I Lie Down to Sleep—1 Minute Total

Location_____ *I did this*___(___Minutes) No___

Desolation From the Day – <u>Write no more than two sentences</u> on what decreased *your faith, your hope, and your love for God and neighbor today.*

Consolation From the Day – <u>Write no more than two sentences</u> on what increased *your faith, your hope, and your love for God and neighbor today.*

SPIRITUAL RECORD

1. Prayer Upon Waking—*I attuned to the day ahead and invited God's help*

Location_____ *I did this*___(___Minutes) No___

2. Exercises During the Day—*Awakening to your life*

Location_____ *I did this*___(___Minutes) No___

3. *Sacred Story* **Prayer Mid-day—***Creation, Presence, Memory, Mercy, Eternity—***15 Minutes Maximum**

Location_____ *I did this*___(___Minutes) No___

4. Exercises During the Day—*Awakening to your life*

Location_____ *I did this*___(___Minutes) No___

5. Prayer upon Retiring—*Attune to your heart, invite God into your dreams*

Location_____ *I did this*___(___Minutes) No___

6. Exercise Journal—1-2 Minutes Once Daily/Weekly/Monthly

Location_____ *I did this*___(___Minutes) No___

7. As I Lie Down to Sleep—1 Minute Total

Location_____ *I did this*___(___Minutes) No___

Write the Month's Most Significant Desolation & Consolation

Desolation From the Day – <u>Write no more than two sentences</u> **on what decreased** *your faith, your hope, and your love for God and neighbor today.*

Consolation From the Day – <u>Write no more than two sentences</u> **on what increased** *your faith, your hope, and your love for God and neighbor today.*

SPIRITUAL RECORD

1. Prayer Upon Waking—*I attuned to the day ahead and invited God's help*

Location_____ *I did this*___(___Minutes) No___

2. Exercises During the Day—*Awakening to your life*

Location_____ *I did this*___(___Minutes) No___

3. *Sacred Story* **Prayer Mid-day—***Creation, Presence, Memory, Mercy,* *Eternity—***15 Minutes Maximum**

Location_____ *I did this*___(___Minutes) No___

4. Exercises During the Day—*Awakening to your life*

Location_____ *I did this*___(___Minutes) No___

5. Prayer upon Retiring—*Attune to your heart, invite God into your dreams*

Location_____ *I did this*___(___Minutes) No___

6. Exercise Journal—1-2 Minutes Once Daily/Weekly/Monthly

Location_____ *I did this*___(___Minutes) No___

7. As I Lie Down to Sleep—1 Minute Total

Location_____ *I did this*___(___Minutes) No___

Desolation From the Day – <u>Write no more than two sentences</u> on what decreased *your faith, your hope, and your love for God and neighbor today.*

Consolation From the Day – <u>Write no more than two sentences</u> on what increased *your faith, your hope, and your love for God and neighbor today.*

SPIRITUAL RECORD

1. Prayer Upon Waking—*I attuned to the day ahead and invited God's help*

Location_____ *I did this*___(___Minutes) No___

2. Exercises During the Day—*Awakening to your life*

Location_____ *I did this*___(___Minutes) No___

3. *Sacred Story* **Prayer Mid-day**—*Creation, Presence, Memory, Mercy,*   *Eternity*—**15 Minutes Maximum**

Location_____ *I did this*___(___Minutes) No___

4. Exercises During the Day—*Awakening to your life*

Location_____ *I did this*___(___Minutes) No___

5. Prayer upon Retiring—*Attune to your heart, invite God into your dreams*

Location_____ *I did this*___(___Minutes) No___

6. Exercise Journal—**1-2 Minutes Once Daily/Weekly/Monthly**

Location_____ *I did this*___(___Minutes) No___

7. As I Lie Down to Sleep—**1 Minute Total**

Location_____ *I did this*___(___Minutes) No___

Desolation From the Day – <u>Write no more than two sentences</u> on what decreased *your faith, your hope, and your love for God and neighbor today.*

Consolation From the Day – <u>Write no more than two sentences</u> on what increased *your faith, your hope, and your love for God and neighbor today.*

SPIRITUAL RECORD

1. Prayer Upon Waking—*I attuned to the day ahead and invited God's help*

Location_____ *I did this*___(___Minutes) No___

2. Exercises During the Day—*Awakening to your life*

Location_____ *I did this*___(___Minutes) No___

3. *Sacred Story* **Prayer Mid-day—***Creation, Presence, Memory, Mercy, Eternity—***15 Minutes Maximum**

Location_____ *I did this*___(___Minutes) No___

4. Exercises During the Day—*Awakening to your life*

Location_____ *I did this*___(___Minutes) No___

5. Prayer upon Retiring—*Attune to your heart, invite God into your dreams*

Location_____ *I did this*___(___Minutes) No___

6. Exercise Journal—1-2 Minutes Once Daily/Weekly/Monthly

Location_____ *I did this*___(___Minutes) No___

7. As I Lie Down to Sleep—1 Minute Total

Location_____ *I did this*___(___Minutes) No___

Desolation From the Day – <u>Write no more than two sentences</u> on what decreased *your faith, your hope, and your love for God and neighbor today.*

Consolation From the Day – <u>Write no more than two sentences</u> on what increased *your faith, your hope, and your love for God and neighbor today.*

SPIRITUAL RECORD

1. Prayer Upon Waking—*I attuned to the day ahead and invited God's help*

Location_____ *I did this*___(___Minutes) No___

2. Exercises During the Day—*Awakening to your life*

Location_____ *I did this*___(___Minutes) No___

3. *Sacred Story* Prayer Mid-day—*Creation, Presence, Memory, Mercy,   Eternity*—15 Minutes Maximum

Location_____ *I did this*___(___Minutes) No___

4. Exercises During the Day—*Awakening to your life*

Location_____ *I did this*___(___Minutes) No___

5. Prayer upon Retiring—*Attune to your heart, invite God into your dreams*

Location_____ *I did this*___(___Minutes) No___

6. Exercise Journal—1-2 Minutes Once Daily/Weekly/Monthly

Location_____ *I did this*___(___Minutes) No___

7. As I Lie Down to Sleep—1 Minute Total

Location_____ *I did this*___(___Minutes) No___

Desolation From the Day – <u>Write no more than two sentences</u> on what decreased *your faith, your hope, and your love for God and neighbor today.*

Consolation From the Day – <u>Write no more than two sentences</u> on what increased *your faith, your hope, and your love for God and neighbor today.*

SPIRITUAL RECORD

1. Prayer Upon Waking—*I attuned to the day ahead and invited God's help*

Location_____ *I did this*___(___Minutes) No___

2. Exercises During the Day—*Awakening to your life*

Location_____ *I did this*___(___Minutes) No___

3. *Sacred Story* **Prayer Mid-day—***Creation, Presence, Memory, Mercy,* *Eternity—***15 Minutes Maximum**

Location_____ *I did this*___(___Minutes) No___

4. Exercises During the Day—*Awakening to your life*

Location_____ *I did this*___(___Minutes) No___

5. Prayer upon Retiring—*Attune to your heart, invite God into your dreams*

Location_____ *I did this*___(___Minutes) No___

6. Exercise Journal—1-2 Minutes Once Daily/Weekly/Monthly

Location_____ *I did this*___(___Minutes) No___

7. As I Lie Down to Sleep—1 Minute Total

Location_____ *I did this*___(___Minutes) No___

Desolation From the Day – <u>Write no more than two sentences</u> on what decreased *your faith, your hope, and your love for God and neighbor today.*

Consolation From the Day – <u>Write no more than two sentences</u> on what increased *your faith, your hope, and your love for God and neighbor today.*

SPIRITUAL RECORD

1. Prayer Upon Waking—*I attuned to the day ahead and invited God's help*

Location_____ *I did this*___(___Minutes) No___

2. Exercises During the Day—*Awakening to your life*

Location_____ *I did this*___(___Minutes) No___

3. *Sacred Story* **Prayer Mid-day—***Creation, Presence, Memory, Mercy,   Eternity—***15 Minutes Maximum**

Location_____ *I did this*___(___Minutes) No___

4. Exercises During the Day—*Awakening to your life*

Location_____ *I did this*___(___Minutes) No___

5. Prayer upon Retiring—*Attune to your heart, invite God into your dreams*

Location_____ *I did this*___(___Minutes) No___

6. Exercise Journal—1-2 Minutes Once Daily/Weekly/Monthly

Location_____ *I did this*___(___Minutes) No___

7. As I Lie Down to Sleep—1 Minute Total

Location_____ *I did this*___(___Minutes) No___

Desolation From the Day – <u>Write no more than two sentences</u> on what decreased *your faith, your hope, and your love for God and neighbor today.*

Consolation From the Day – <u>Write no more than two sentences</u> on what increased *your faith, your hope, and your love for God and neighbor today.*

SPIRITUAL RECORD

1. Prayer Upon Waking—*I attuned to the day ahead and invited God's help*

Location_____ *I did this*___(___Minutes) No___

2. Exercises During the Day—*Awakening to your life*

Location_____ *I did this*___(___Minutes) No___

3. *Sacred Story* Prayer Mid-day—*Creation, Presence, Memory, Mercy, Eternity*—**15 Minutes Maximum**

Location_____ *I did this*___(___Minutes) No___

4. Exercises During the Day—*Awakening to your life*

Location_____ *I did this*___(___Minutes) No___

5. Prayer upon Retiring—*Attune to your heart, invite God into your dreams*

Location_____ *I did this*___(___Minutes) No___

6. Exercise Journal—1-2 Minutes Once Daily/Weekly/Monthly

Location_____ *I did this*___(___Minutes) No___

7. As I Lie Down to Sleep—1 Minute Total

Location_____ *I did this*___(___Minutes) No___

Write the Week's Most Significant Desolation & Consolation

Desolation From the Day – Write no more than two sentences **on what decreased** *your faith, your hope, and your love for God and neighbor today.*

Consolation From the Day – Write no more than two sentences **on what increased** *your faith, your hope, and your love for God and neighbor today.*

 # Week 30

SPIRITUAL RECORD

1. Prayer Upon Waking—*I attuned to the day ahead and invited God's help*

Location_____ *I did this*___(___Minutes) No___

2. Exercises During the Day—*Awakening to your life*

Location_____ *I did this*___(___Minutes) No___

3. *Sacred Story* Prayer Mid-day—*Creation, Presence, Memory, Mercy,* *Eternity*—15 Minutes Maximum

Location_____ *I did this*___(___Minutes) No___

4. Exercises During the Day—*Awakening to your life*

Location_____ *I did this*___(___Minutes) No___

5. Prayer upon Retiring—*Attune to your heart, invite God into your dreams*

Location_____ *I did this*___(___Minutes) No___

6. Exercise Journal—1-2 Minutes Once Daily/Weekly/Monthly

Location_____ *I did this*___(___Minutes) No___

7. As I Lie Down to Sleep—1 Minute Total

Location_____ *I did this*___(___Minutes) No___

Desolation From the Day – <u>Write no more than two sentences</u> on what decreased *your faith, your hope, and your love for God and neighbor today.*

Consolation From the Day – <u>Write no more than two sentences</u> on what increased *your faith, your hope, and your love for God and neighbor today.*

SPIRITUAL RECORD

1. Prayer Upon Waking—*I attuned to the day ahead and invited God's help*

Location_____ *I did this*___(___Minutes) No___

2. Exercises During the Day—*Awakening to your life*

Location_____ *I did this*___(___Minutes) No___

3. *Sacred Story* Prayer Mid-day—*Creation, Presence, Memory, Mercy,   Eternity*—15 Minutes Maximum

Location_____ *I did this*___(___Minutes) No___

4. Exercises During the Day—*Awakening to your life*

Location_____ *I did this*___(___Minutes) No___

5. Prayer upon Retiring—*Attune to your heart, invite God into your dreams*

Location_____ *I did this*___(___Minutes) No___

6. Exercise Journal—1-2 Minutes Once Daily/Weekly/Monthly

Location_____ *I did this*___(___Minutes) No___

7. As I Lie Down to Sleep—1 Minute Total

Location_____ *I did this*___(___Minutes) No___

Desolation From the Day – <u>Write no more than two sentences</u> on what decreased *your faith, your hope, and your love for God and neighbor today.*

Consolation From the Day – <u>Write no more than two sentences</u> on what increased *your faith, your hope, and your love for God and neighbor today.*

SPIRITUAL RECORD

1. Prayer Upon Waking—*I attuned to the day ahead and invited God's help*

Location_____ *I did this*___(___Minutes) No___

2. Exercises During the Day—*Awakening to your life*

Location_____ *I did this*___(___Minutes) No___

3. *Sacred Story* **Prayer Mid-day—***Creation, Presence, Memory, Mercy,* *Eternity—***15 Minutes Maximum**

Location_____ *I did this*___(___Minutes) No___

4. Exercises During the Day—*Awakening to your life*

Location_____ *I did this*___(___Minutes) No___

5. Prayer upon Retiring—*Attune to your heart, invite God into your dreams*

Location_____ *I did this*___(___Minutes) No___

6. Exercise Journal—1-2 Minutes Once Daily/Weekly/Monthly

Location_____ *I did this*___(___Minutes) No___

7. As I Lie Down to Sleep—1 Minute Total

Location_____ *I did this*___(___Minutes) No___

Desolation From the Day – <u>Write no more than two sentences</u> on what decreased *your faith, your hope, and your love for God and neighbor today.*

Consolation From the Day – <u>Write no more than two sentences</u> on what increased *your faith, your hope, and your love for God and neighbor today.*

SPIRITUAL RECORD

1. Prayer Upon Waking—*I attuned to the day ahead and invited God's help*

Location_____ *I did this___(___Minutes) No___*

2. Exercises During the Day—*Awakening to your life*

Location_____ *I did this___(___Minutes) No___*

3. *Sacred Story* Prayer Mid-day—*Creation, Presence, Memory, Mercy,*   *Eternity*—15 Minutes Maximum

Location_____ *I did this___(___Minutes) No___*

4. Exercises During the Day—*Awakening to your life*

Location_____ *I did this___(___Minutes) No___*

5. Prayer upon Retiring—*Attune to your heart, invite God into your dreams*

Location_____ *I did this___(___Minutes) No___*

6. Exercise Journal—1-2 Minutes Once Daily/Weekly/Monthly

Location_____ *I did this___(___Minutes) No___*

7. As I Lie Down to Sleep—1 Minute Total

Location_____ *I did this___(___Minutes) No___*

Desolation From the Day – <u>Write no more than two sentences</u> on what decreased *your faith, your hope, and your love for God and neighbor today.*

Consolation From the Day – <u>Write no more than two sentences</u> on what increased *your faith, your hope, and your love for God and neighbor today.*

SPIRITUAL RECORD

1. Prayer Upon Waking—*I attuned to the day ahead and invited God's help*

Location_____   *I did this*___(___Minutes) No___

2. Exercises During the Day—*Awakening to your life*

Location_____   *I did this*___(___Minutes) No___

3. *Sacred Story* **Prayer Mid-day**—*Creation, Presence, Memory, Mercy,   Eternity*—15 **Minutes Maximum**

Location_____   *I did this*___(___Minutes) No___

4. Exercises During the Day—*Awakening to your life*

Location_____   *I did this*___(___Minutes) No___

5. Prayer upon Retiring—*Attune to your heart, invite God into your dreams*

Location_____   *I did this*___(___Minutes) No___

6. Exercise Journal—**1-2 Minutes Once Daily/Weekly/Monthly**

Location_____   *I did this*___(___Minutes) No___

7. As I Lie Down to Sleep—**1 Minute Total**

Location_____   *I did this*___(___Minutes) No___

Desolation From the Day – <u>Write no more than two sentences</u> on what decreased *your faith, your hope, and your love for God and neighbor today.*

Consolation From the Day – <u>Write no more than two sentences</u> on what increased *your faith, your hope, and your love for God and neighbor today.*

SPIRITUAL RECORD

1. Prayer Upon Waking—*I attuned to the day ahead and invited God's help*

Location_____ *I did this*___(___Minutes) No___

2. Exercises During the Day—*Awakening to your life*

Location_____ *I did this*___(___Minutes) No___

3. *Sacred Story* **Prayer Mid-day**—*Creation, Presence, Memory, Mercy,* *Eternity*—15 **Minutes Maximum**

Location_____ *I did this*___(___Minutes) No___

4. Exercises During the Day—*Awakening to your life*

Location_____ *I did this*___(___Minutes) No___

5. Prayer upon Retiring—*Attune to your heart, invite God into your dreams*

Location_____ *I did this*___(___Minutes) No___

6. Exercise Journal—**1-2 Minutes Once Daily/Weekly/Monthly**

Location_____ *I did this*___(___Minutes) No___

7. As I Lie Down to Sleep—**1 Minute Total**

Location_____ *I did this*___(___Minutes) No___

Desolation From the Day – <u>Write no more than two sentences</u> on what decreased *your faith, your hope, and your love for God and neighbor today.*

Consolation From the Day – <u>Write no more than two sentences</u> on what increased *your faith, your hope, and your love for God and neighbor today.*

SPIRITUAL RECORD

1. Prayer Upon Waking—*I attuned to the day ahead and invited God's help*

Location_____ *I did this___(___*Minutes) No___

2. Exercises During the Day—*Awakening to your life*

Location_____ *I did this___(___*Minutes) No___

3. *Sacred Story* **Prayer Mid-day—***Creation, Presence, Memory, Mercy,   Eternity—***15 Minutes Maximum**

Location_____ *I did this___(___*Minutes) No___

4. Exercises During the Day—*Awakening to your life*

Location_____ *I did this___(___*Minutes) No___

5. Prayer upon Retiring—*Attune to your heart, invite God into your dreams*

Location_____ *I did this___(___*Minutes) No___

6. Exercise Journal—1-2 Minutes Once Daily/Weekly/Monthly

Location_____ *I did this___(___*Minutes) No___

7. As I Lie Down to Sleep—1 Minute Total

Location_____ *I did this___(___*Minutes) No___

Write the Week's Most Significant Desolation & Consolation

Desolation From the Day – **<u>Write no more than two sentences</u> on what decreased *your faith, your hope, and your love for God and neighbor today.*

Consolation From the Day – **<u>Write no more than two sentences</u> on what increased *your faith, your hope, and your love for God and neighbor today.*

 Week 31

SPIRITUAL RECORD

1. Prayer Upon Waking—*I attuned to the day ahead and invited God's help*

Location_____ *I did this*___(___Minutes) No___

2. Exercises During the Day—*Awakening to your life*

Location_____ *I did this*___(___Minutes) No___

3. *Sacred Story* **Prayer Mid-day—***Creation, Presence, Memory, Mercy,   Eternity—***15 Minutes Maximum**

Location_____ *I did this*___(___Minutes) No___

4. Exercises During the Day—*Awakening to your life*

Location_____ *I did this*___(___Minutes) No___

5. Prayer upon Retiring—*Attune to your heart, invite God into your dreams*

Location_____ *I did this*___(___Minutes) No___

6. Exercise Journal—1-2 Minutes Once Daily/Weekly/Monthly

Location_____ *I did this*___(___Minutes) No___

7. As I Lie Down to Sleep—1 Minute Total

Location_____ *I did this*___(___Minutes) No___

Desolation From the Day – Write no more than two sentences on what decreased *your faith, your hope, and your love for God and neighbor today.*

Consolation From the Day – Write no more than two sentences on what increased *your faith, your hope, and your love for God and neighbor today.*

SPIRITUAL RECORD

1. Prayer Upon Waking—*I attuned to the day ahead and invited God's help*

Location_____ *I did this*___(___Minutes) No___

2. Exercises During the Day—*Awakening to your life*

Location_____ *I did this*___(___Minutes) No___

3. *Sacred Story* Prayer Mid-day—*Creation, Presence, Memory, Mercy,   Eternity*—15 Minutes Maximum

Location_____ *I did this*___(___Minutes) No___

4. Exercises During the Day—*Awakening to your life*

Location_____ *I did this*___(___Minutes) No___

5. Prayer upon Retiring—*Attune to your heart, invite God into your dreams*

Location_____ *I did this*___(___Minutes) No___

6. Exercise Journal—1-2 Minutes Once Daily/Weekly/Monthly

Location_____ *I did this*___(___Minutes) No___

7. As I Lie Down to Sleep—1 Minute Total

Location_____ *I did this*___(___Minutes) No___

Desolation From the Day – <u>Write no more than two sentences</u> on what decreased *your faith, your hope, and your love for God and neighbor today.*

Consolation From the Day – <u>Write no more than two sentences</u> on what increased *your faith, your hope, and your love for God and neighbor today.*

SPIRITUAL RECORD

1. Prayer Upon Waking—*I attuned to the day ahead and invited God's help*

Location_____ *I did this*____(____Minutes) No____

2. Exercises During the Day—*Awakening to your life*

Location_____ *I did this*____(____Minutes) No____

3. *Sacred Story* Prayer Mid-day—*Creation, Presence, Memory, Mercy,*   *Eternity—15* **Minutes Maximum**

Location_____ *I did this*____(____Minutes) No____

4. Exercises During the Day—*Awakening to your life*

Location_____ *I did this*____(____Minutes) No____

5. Prayer upon Retiring—*Attune to your heart, invite God into your dreams*

Location_____ *I did this*____(____Minutes) No____

6. Exercise Journal—1-2 Minutes Once Daily/Weekly/Monthly

Location_____ *I did this*____(____Minutes) No____

7. As I Lie Down to Sleep—1 Minute Total

Location_____ *I did this*____(____Minutes) No____

Desolation From the Day – <u>Write no more than two sentences</u> on what decreased *your faith, your hope, and your love for God and neighbor today.*

Consolation From the Day – <u>Write no more than two sentences</u> on what increased *your faith, your hope, and your love for God and neighbor today.*

217

SPIRITUAL RECORD

1. Prayer Upon Waking—*I attuned to the day ahead and invited God's help*

Location_____ *I did this*___(___Minutes) No___

2. Exercises During the Day—*Awakening to your life*

Location_____ *I did this*___(___Minutes) No___

3. *Sacred Story* Prayer Mid-day—*Creation, Presence, Memory, Mercy, Eternity*—15 Minutes Maximum

Location_____ *I did this*___(___Minutes) No___

4. Exercises During the Day—*Awakening to your life*

Location_____ *I did this*___(___Minutes) No___

5. Prayer upon Retiring—*Attune to your heart, invite God into your dreams*

Location_____ *I did this*___(___Minutes) No___

6. Exercise Journal—1-2 Minutes Once Daily/Weekly/Monthly

Location_____ *I did this*___(___Minutes) No___

7. As I Lie Down to Sleep—1 Minute Total

Location_____ *I did this*___(___Minutes) No___

Desolation From the Day – <u>Write no more than two sentences</u> on what decreased *your faith, your hope, and your love for God and neighbor today.*

Consolation From the Day – <u>Write no more than two sentences</u> on what increased *your faith, your hope, and your love for God and neighbor today.*

SPIRITUAL RECORD

1. Prayer Upon Waking—*I attuned to the day ahead and invited God's help*

Location_____ *I did this*___(___Minutes) No___

2. Exercises During the Day—*Awakening to your life*

Location_____ *I did this*___(___Minutes) No___

3. *Sacred Story* **Prayer Mid-day**—*Creation, Presence, Memory, Mercy,   Eternity*—**15 Minutes Maximum**

Location_____ *I did this*___(___Minutes) No___

4. Exercises During the Day—*Awakening to your life*

Location_____ *I did this*___(___Minutes) No___

5. Prayer upon Retiring—*Attune to your heart, invite God into your dreams*

Location_____ *I did this*___(___Minutes) No___

6. Exercise Journal—**1-2 Minutes Once Daily/Weekly/Monthly**

Location_____ *I did this*___(___Minutes) No___

7. As I Lie Down to Sleep—**1 Minute Total**

Location_____ *I did this*___(___Minutes) No___

Desolation From the Day – Write no more than two sentences on what decreased *your faith, your hope, and your love for God and neighbor today.*

Consolation From the Day – Write no more than two sentences on what increased *your faith, your hope, and your love for God and neighbor today.*

SPIRITUAL RECORD

1. Prayer Upon Waking—*I attuned to the day ahead and invited God's help*

Location_____ *I did this*___(___Minutes) No___

2. Exercises During the Day—*Awakening to your life*

Location_____ *I did this*___(___Minutes) No___

3. *Sacred Story* Prayer Mid-day—*Creation, Presence, Memory, Mercy, Eternity*—15 Minutes Maximum

Location_____ *I did this*___(___Minutes) No___

4. Exercises During the Day—*Awakening to your life*

Location_____ *I did this*___(___Minutes) No___

5. Prayer upon Retiring—*Attune to your heart, invite God into your dreams*

Location_____ *I did this*___(___Minutes) No___

6. Exercise Journal—1-2 Minutes Once Daily/Weekly/Monthly

Location_____ *I did this*___(___Minutes) No___

7. As I Lie Down to Sleep—1 Minute Total

Location_____ *I did this*___(___Minutes) No___

Desolation From the Day – <u>Write no more than two sentences</u> on what decreased *your faith, your hope, and your love for God and neighbor today.*

Consolation From the Day – <u>Write no more than two sentences</u> on what increased *your faith, your hope, and your love for God and neighbor today.*

SPIRITUAL RECORD

1. Prayer Upon Waking—*I attuned to the day ahead and invited God's help*

Location_____ *I did this*___(___Minutes) No___

2. Exercises During the Day—*Awakening to your life*

Location_____ *I did this*___(___Minutes) No___

3. *Sacred Story* Prayer Mid-day—*Creation, Presence, Memory, Mercy,   Eternity*—15 **Minutes Maximum**

Location_____ *I did this*___(___Minutes) No___

4. Exercises During the Day—*Awakening to your life*

Location_____ *I did this*___(___Minutes) No___

5. Prayer upon Retiring—*Attune to your heart, invite God into your dreams*

Location_____ *I did this*___(___Minutes) No___

6. Exercise Journal—**1-2 Minutes Once Daily/Weekly/Monthly**

Location_____ *I did this*___(___Minutes) No___

7. As I Lie Down to Sleep—**1 Minute Total**

Location_____ *I did this*___(___Minutes) No___

Write the Week's Most Significant Desolation & Consolation

Desolation From the Day – <u>Write no more than two sentences</u> on what decreased *your faith, your hope, and your love for God and neighbor today.*

Consolation From the Day – <u>Write no more than two sentences</u> on what increased *your faith, your hope, and your love for God and neighbor today.*

Week 32

SPIRITUAL RECORD

1. Prayer Upon Waking—*I attuned to the day ahead and invited God's help*

Location_____ *I did this*___(___Minutes) No___

2. Exercises During the Day—*Awakening to your life*

Location_____ *I did this*___(___Minutes) No___

3. *Sacred Story* Prayer Mid-day—*Creation, Presence, Memory, Mercy,   Eternity*—15 Minutes Maximum

Location_____ *I did this*___(___Minutes) No___

4. Exercises During the Day—*Awakening to your life*

Location_____ *I did this*___(___Minutes) No___

5. Prayer upon Retiring—*Attune to your heart, invite God into your dreams*

Location_____ *I did this*___(___Minutes) No___

6. Exercise Journal—1-2 Minutes Once Daily/Weekly/Monthly

Location_____ *I did this*___(___Minutes) No___

7. As I Lie Down to Sleep—1 Minute Total

Location_____ *I did this*___(___Minutes) No___

Desolation From the Day – <u>Write no more than two sentences</u> on what decreased *your faith, your hope, and your love for God and neighbor today.*

Consolation From the Day – <u>Write no more than two sentences</u> on what increased *your faith, your hope, and your love for God and neighbor today.*

SPIRITUAL RECORD

1. Prayer Upon Waking—*I attuned to the day ahead and invited God's help*

Location_____ *I did this___(___Minutes)* No___

2. Exercises During the Day—*Awakening to your life*

Location_____ *I did this___(___Minutes)* No___

3. *Sacred Story* Prayer Mid-day—*Creation, Presence, Memory, Mercy,*   *Eternity*—15 Minutes Maximum

Location_____ *I did this___(___Minutes)* No___

4. Exercises During the Day—*Awakening to your life*

Location_____ *I did this___(___Minutes)* No___

5. Prayer upon Retiring—*Attune to your heart, invite God into your dreams*

Location_____ *I did this___(___Minutes)* No___

6. Exercise Journal—1-2 Minutes Once Daily/Weekly/Monthly

Location_____ *I did this___(___Minutes)* No___

7. As I Lie Down to Sleep—1 Minute Total

Location_____ *I did this___(___Minutes)* No___

Desolation From the Day – <u>Write no more than two sentences</u> on what decreased *your faith, your hope, and your love for God and neighbor today.*

Consolation From the Day – <u>Write no more than two sentences</u> on what increased *your faith, your hope, and your love for God and neighbor today.*

SPIRITUAL RECORD

1. Prayer Upon Waking—*I attuned to the day ahead and invited God's help*

Location_____   *I did this*___(___Minutes) No___

2. Exercises During the Day—*Awakening to your life*

Location_____   *I did this*___(___Minutes) No___

3. *Sacred Story* **Prayer Mid-day**—*Creation, Presence, Memory, Mercy,   Eternity*—**15 Minutes Maximum**

Location_____   *I did this*___(___Minutes) No___

4. Exercises During the Day—*Awakening to your life*

Location_____   *I did this*___(___Minutes) No___

5. Prayer upon Retiring—*Attune to your heart, invite God into your dreams*

Location_____   *I did this*___(___Minutes) No___

6. Exercise Journal—1-2 Minutes Once Daily/Weekly/Monthly

Location_____   *I did this*___(___Minutes) No___

7. As I Lie Down to Sleep—1 Minute Total

Location_____   *I did this*___(___Minutes) No___

Desolation From the Day – Write no more than two sentences on what decreased *your faith, your hope, and your love for God and neighbor today.*

Consolation From the Day – Write no more than two sentences on what increased *your faith, your hope, and your love for God and neighbor today.*

SPIRITUAL RECORD

1. Prayer Upon Waking—*I attuned to the day ahead and invited God's help*

Location_____   *I did this*____(____Minutes) No____

2. Exercises During the Day—*Awakening to your life*

Location_____   *I did this*____(____Minutes) No____

3. *Sacred Story* **Prayer Mid-day—***Creation, Presence, Memory, Mercy,*   *Eternity—***15 Minutes Maximum**

Location_____   *I did this*____(____Minutes) No____

4. Exercises During the Day—*Awakening to your life*

Location_____   *I did this*____(____Minutes) No____

5. Prayer upon Retiring—*Attune to your heart, invite God into your dreams*

Location_____   *I did this*____(____Minutes) No____

6. Exercise Journal—1-2 Minutes Once Daily/Weekly/Monthly

Location_____   *I did this*____(____Minutes) No____

7. As I Lie Down to Sleep—1 Minute Total

Location_____   *I did this*____(____Minutes) No____

Desolation From the Day – <u>Write no more than two sentences</u> on what decreased *your faith, your hope, and your love for God and neighbor today.*

Consolation From the Day – <u>Write no more than two sentences</u> on what increased *your faith, your hope, and your love for God and neighbor today.*

SPIRITUAL RECORD

1. Prayer Upon Waking—*I attuned to the day ahead and invited God's help*

Location_____ *I did this*___(___Minutes) No___

2. Exercises During the Day—*Awakening to your life*

Location_____ *I did this*___(___Minutes) No___

3. *Sacred Story* Prayer Mid-day—*Creation, Presence, Memory, Mercy,   Eternity*—15 Minutes Maximum

Location_____ *I did this*___(___Minutes) No___

4. Exercises During the Day—*Awakening to your life*

Location_____ *I did this*___(___Minutes) No___

5. Prayer upon Retiring—*Attune to your heart, invite God into your dreams*

Location_____ *I did this*___(___Minutes) No___

6. Exercise Journal—1-2 Minutes Once Daily/Weekly/Monthly

Location_____ *I did this*___(___Minutes) No___

7. As I Lie Down to Sleep—1 Minute Total

Location_____ *I did this*___(___Minutes) No___

Desolation From the Day – <u>Write no more than two sentences</u> on what decreased *your faith, your hope, and your love for God and neighbor today.*

Consolation From the Day – <u>Write no more than two sentences</u> on what increased *your faith, your hope, and your love for God and neighbor today.*

SPIRITUAL RECORD

1. Prayer Upon Waking—*I attuned to the day ahead and invited God's help*

Location_____ *I did this*___(___Minutes) No___

2. Exercises During the Day—*Awakening to your life*

Location_____ *I did this*___(___Minutes) No___

3. *Sacred Story* **Prayer Mid-day—***Creation, Presence, Memory, Mercy,* *Eternity—***15 Minutes Maximum**

Location_____ *I did this*___(___Minutes) No___

4. Exercises During the Day—*Awakening to your life*

Location_____ *I did this*___(___Minutes) No___

5. Prayer upon Retiring—*Attune to your heart, invite God into your dreams*

Location_____ *I did this*___(___Minutes) No___

6. Exercise Journal—1-2 Minutes Once Daily/Weekly/Monthly

Location_____ *I did this*___(___Minutes) No___

7. As I Lie Down to Sleep—1 Minute Total

Location_____ *I did this*___(___Minutes) No___

Desolation From the Day – <u>Write no more than two sentences</u> on what decreased *your faith, your hope, and your love for God and neighbor today.*

Consolation From the Day – <u>Write no more than two sentences</u> on what increased *your faith, your hope, and your love for God and neighbor today.*

SPIRITUAL RECORD

1. Prayer Upon Waking—*I attuned to the day ahead and invited God's help*

Location_____ *I did this*___(___Minutes) No___

2. Exercises During the Day—*Awakening to your life*

Location_____ *I did this*___(___Minutes) No___

3. *Sacred Story* Prayer Mid-day—*Creation, Presence, Memory, Mercy, Eternity*—15 Minutes Maximum

Location_____ *I did this*___(___Minutes) No___

4. Exercises During the Day—*Awakening to your life*

Location_____ *I did this*___(___Minutes) No___

5. Prayer upon Retiring—*Attune to your heart, invite God into your dreams*

Location_____ *I did this*___(___Minutes) No___

6. Exercise Journal—1-2 Minutes Once Daily/Weekly/Monthly

Location_____ *I did this*___(___Minutes) No___

7. As I Lie Down to Sleep—1 Minute Total

Location_____ *I did this*___(___Minutes) No___

Write the Month's Most Significant Desolation & Consolation

Desolation From the Day – <u>Write no more than two sentences</u> on what decreased *your faith, your hope, and your love for God and neighbor today.*

Consolation From the Day – <u>Write no more than two sentences</u> on what increased *your faith, your hope, and your love for God and neighbor today.*

Week 33

SPIRITUAL RECORD

1. Prayer Upon Waking—*I attuned to the day ahead and invited God's help*

Location_____ *I did this___(___Minutes)* No___

2. Exercises During the Day—*Awakening to your life*

Location_____ *I did this___(___Minutes)* No___

3. *Sacred Story* **Prayer Mid-day—***Creation, Presence, Memory, Mercy,* **Eternity—15 Minutes Maximum**

Location_____ *I did this___(___Minutes)* No___

4. Exercises During the Day—*Awakening to your life*

Location_____ *I did this___(___Minutes)* No___

5. Prayer upon Retiring—*Attune to your heart, invite God into your dreams*

Location_____ *I did this___(___Minutes)* No___

6. Exercise Journal—1-2 Minutes Once Daily/Weekly/Monthly

Location_____ *I did this___(___Minutes)* No___

7. As I Lie Down to Sleep—1 Minute Total

Location_____ *I did this___(___Minutes)* No___

Desolation From the Day – <u>Write no more than two sentences</u> on what decreased *your faith, your hope, and your love for God and neighbor today.*

Consolation From the Day – <u>Write no more than two sentences</u> on what increased *your faith, your hope, and your love for God and neighbor today.*

SPIRITUAL RECORD

1. Prayer Upon Waking—*I attuned to the day ahead and invited God's help*

Location_____   *I did this*___(___Minutes) No___

2. Exercises During the Day—*Awakening to your life*

Location_____   *I did this*___(___Minutes) No___

3. *Sacred Story* **Prayer Mid-day**—*Creation, Presence, Memory, Mercy,   Eternity*—15 **Minutes Maximum**

Location_____   *I did this*___(___Minutes) No___

4. Exercises During the Day—*Awakening to your life*

Location_____   *I did this*___(___Minutes) No___

5. Prayer upon Retiring—*Attune to your heart, invite God into your dreams*

Location_____   *I did this*___(___Minutes) No___

6. Exercise Journal—**1-2 Minutes Once Daily/Weekly/Monthly**

Location_____   *I did this*___(___Minutes) No___

7. As I Lie Down to Sleep—**1 Minute Total**

Location_____   *I did this*___(___Minutes) No___

Desolation From the Day – <u>Write no more than two sentences</u> on what decreased *your faith, your hope, and your love for God and neighbor today.*

Consolation From the Day – <u>Write no more than two sentences</u> on what increased *your faith, your hope, and your love for God and neighbor today.*

SPIRITUAL RECORD

1. Prayer Upon Waking—*I attuned to the day ahead and invited God's help*

Location_____ *I did this*___(___Minutes) No___

2. Exercises During the Day—*Awakening to your life*

Location_____ *I did this*___(___Minutes) No___

3. *Sacred Story* Prayer Mid-day—*Creation, Presence, Memory, Mercy,* Eternity—15 Minutes Maximum

Location_____ *I did this*___(___Minutes) No___

4. Exercises During the Day—*Awakening to your life*

Location_____ *I did this*___(___Minutes) No___

5. Prayer upon Retiring—*Attune to your heart, invite God into your dreams*

Location_____ *I did this*___(___Minutes) No___

6. Exercise Journal—1-2 Minutes Once Daily/Weekly/Monthly

Location_____ *I did this*___(___Minutes) No___

7. As I Lie Down to Sleep—1 Minute Total

Location_____ *I did this*___(___Minutes) No___

Desolation From the Day – <u>Write no more than two sentences</u> on what decreased *your faith, your hope, and your love for God and neighbor today.*

Consolation From the Day – <u>Write no more than two sentences</u> on what increased *your faith, your hope, and your love for God and neighbor today.*

SPIRITUAL RECORD

1. Prayer Upon Waking—*I attuned to the day ahead and invited God's help*

Location_____ *I did this*___(___Minutes) No___

2. Exercises During the Day—*Awakening to your life*

Location_____ *I did this*___(___Minutes) No___

3. *Sacred Story* Prayer Mid-day—*Creation, Presence, Memory, Mercy,* *Eternity*—**15 Minutes Maximum**

Location_____ *I did this*___(___Minutes) No___

4. Exercises During the Day—*Awakening to your life*

Location_____ *I did this*___(___Minutes) No___

5. Prayer upon Retiring—*Attune to your heart, invite God into your dreams*

Location_____ *I did this*___(___Minutes) No___

6. Exercise Journal—1-2 Minutes Once Daily/Weekly/Monthly

Location_____ *I did this*___(___Minutes) No___

7. As I Lie Down to Sleep—1 Minute Total

Location_____ *I did this*___(___Minutes) No___

Desolation From the Day – <u>Write no more than two sentences</u> on what decreased *your faith, your hope, and your love for God and neighbor today.*

Consolation From the Day – <u>Write no more than two sentences</u> on what increased *your faith, your hope, and your love for God and neighbor today.*

SPIRITUAL RECORD

1. Prayer Upon Waking—*I attuned to the day ahead and invited God's help*

Location_____ *I did this*___(___Minutes) No___

2. Exercises During the Day—*Awakening to your life*

Location_____ *I did this*___(___Minutes) No___

3. *Sacred Story* **Prayer Mid-day—***Creation, Presence, Memory, Mercy,*   *Eternity—***15 Minutes Maximum**

Location_____ *I did this*___(___Minutes) No___

4. Exercises During the Day—*Awakening to your life*

Location_____ *I did this*___(___Minutes) No___

5. Prayer upon Retiring—*Attune to your heart, invite God into your dreams*

Location_____ *I did this*___(___Minutes) No___

6. Exercise Journal—1-2 Minutes Once Daily/Weekly/Monthly

Location_____ *I did this*___(___Minutes) No___

7. As I Lie Down to Sleep—1 Minute Total

Location_____ *I did this*___(___Minutes) No___

Desolation From the Day – <u>Write no more than two sentences</u> on what decreased *your faith, your hope, and your love for God and neighbor today.*

Consolation From the Day – <u>Write no more than two sentences</u> on what increased *your faith, your hope, and your love for God and neighbor today.*

SPIRITUAL RECORD

1. Prayer Upon Waking—*I attuned to the day ahead and invited God's help*

Location_____ *I did this*___(___Minutes) No___

2. Exercises During the Day—*Awakening to your life*

Location_____ *I did this*___(___Minutes) No___

3. *Sacred Story* Prayer Mid-day—*Creation, Presence, Memory, Mercy,   Eternity*—15 Minutes Maximum

Location_____ *I did this*___(___Minutes) No___

4. Exercises During the Day—*Awakening to your life*

Location_____ *I did this*___(___Minutes) No___

5. Prayer upon Retiring—*Attune to your heart, invite God into your dreams*

Location_____ *I did this*___(___Minutes) No___

6. Exercise Journal—1-2 Minutes Once Daily/Weekly/Monthly

Location_____ *I did this*___(___Minutes) No___

7. As I Lie Down to Sleep—1 Minute Total

Location_____ *I did this*___(___Minutes) No___

Desolation From the Day – <u>Write no more than two sentences</u> on what decreased *your faith, your hope, and your love for God and neighbor today.*

Consolation From the Day – <u>Write no more than two sentences</u> on what increased *your faith, your hope, and your love for God and neighbor today.*

SPIRITUAL RECORD

1. Prayer Upon Waking—*I attuned to the day ahead and invited God's help*

Location_____   *I did this*___(___Minutes) No___

2. Exercises During the Day—*Awakening to your life*

Location_____   *I did this*___(___Minutes) No___

3. *Sacred Story* Prayer Mid-day—*Creation, Presence, Memory, Mercy,*   *Eternity—***15 Minutes Maximum**

Location_____   *I did this*___(___Minutes) No___

4. Exercises During the Day—*Awakening to your life*

Location_____   *I did this*___(___Minutes) No___

5. Prayer upon Retiring—*Attune to your heart, invite God into your dreams*

Location_____   *I did this*___(___Minutes) No___

6. Exercise Journal—1-2 Minutes Once Daily/Weekly/Monthly

Location_____   *I did this*___(___Minutes) No___

7. As I Lie Down to Sleep—1 Minute Total

Location_____   *I did this*___(___Minutes) No___

Write the Week's Most Significant Desolation & Consolation

Desolation From the Day – <u>Write no more than two sentences</u> on what decreased *your faith, your hope, and your love for God and neighbor today.*

Consolation From the Day – <u>Write no more than two sentences</u> on what increased *your faith, your hope, and your love for God and neighbor today.*

 # Week 34

SPIRITUAL RECORD

1. Prayer Upon Waking—*I attuned to the day ahead and invited God's help*

Location_____ *I did this*___(___Minutes) No___

2. Exercises During the Day—*Awakening to your life*

Location_____ *I did this*___(___Minutes) No___

3. *Sacred Story* Prayer Mid-day—*Creation, Presence, Memory, Mercy,   Eternity*—15 Minutes Maximum

Location_____ *I did this*___(___Minutes) No___

4. Exercises During the Day—*Awakening to your life*

Location_____ *I did this*___(___Minutes) No___

5. Prayer upon Retiring—*Attune to your heart, invite God into your dreams*

Location_____ *I did this*___(___Minutes) No___

6. Exercise Journal—1-2 Minutes Once Daily/Weekly/Monthly

Location_____ *I did this*___(___Minutes) No___

7. As I Lie Down to Sleep—1 Minute Total

Location_____ *I did this*___(___Minutes) No___

Desolation From the Day – <u>Write no more than two sentences</u> on what decreased *your faith, your hope, and your love for God and neighbor today.*

Consolation From the Day – <u>Write no more than two sentences</u> on what increased *your faith, your hope, and your love for God and neighbor today.*

236

SPIRITUAL RECORD

1. Prayer Upon Waking—*I attuned to the day ahead and invited God's help*

Location_____   *I did this*___(___Minutes) No___

2. Exercises During the Day—*Awakening to your life*

Location_____   *I did this*___(___Minutes) No___

3. *Sacred Story* Prayer Mid-day—*Creation, Presence, Memory, Mercy,*   *Eternity*—15 Minutes Maximum

Location_____   *I did this*___(___Minutes) No___

4. Exercises During the Day—*Awakening to your life*

Location_____   *I did this*___(___Minutes) No___

5. Prayer upon Retiring—*Attune to your heart, invite God into your dreams*

Location_____   *I did this*___(___Minutes) No___

6. Exercise Journal—1-2 Minutes Once Daily/Weekly/Monthly

Location_____   *I did this*___(___Minutes) No___

7. As I Lie Down to Sleep—1 Minute Total

Location_____   *I did this*___(___Minutes) No___

Desolation From the Day – <u>Write no more than two sentences</u> on what decreased *your faith, your hope, and your love for God and neighbor today.*

Consolation From the Day – <u>Write no more than two sentences</u> on what increased *your faith, your hope, and your love for God and neighbor today.*

SPIRITUAL RECORD

1. Prayer Upon Waking—*I attuned to the day ahead and invited God's help*

Location_____ *I did this*___(___Minutes) No___

2. Exercises During the Day—*Awakening to your life*

Location_____ *I did this*___(___Minutes) No___

3. *Sacred Story* **Prayer Mid-day—***Creation, Presence, Memory, Mercy,   Eternity—***15 Minutes Maximum**

Location_____ *I did this*___(___Minutes) No___

4. Exercises During the Day—*Awakening to your life*

Location_____ *I did this*___(___Minutes) No___

5. Prayer upon Retiring—*Attune to your heart, invite God into your dreams*

Location_____ *I did this*___(___Minutes) No___

6. Exercise Journal—1-2 Minutes Once Daily/Weekly/Monthly

Location_____ *I did this*___(___Minutes) No___

7. As I Lie Down to Sleep—1 Minute Total

Location_____ *I did this*___(___Minutes) No___

Desolation From the Day – <u>Write no more than two sentences</u> on what decreased *your faith, your hope, and your love for God and neighbor today.*

Consolation From the Day – <u>Write no more than two sentences</u> on what increased *your faith, your hope, and your love for God and neighbor today.*

SPIRITUAL RECORD

1. Prayer Upon Waking—*I attuned to the day ahead and invited God's help*

Location_____ *I did this*___(___Minutes) No___

2. Exercises During the Day—*Awakening to your life*

Location_____ *I did this*___(___Minutes) No___

3. *Sacred Story* Prayer Mid-day—*Creation, Presence, Memory, Mercy, Eternity*—15 Minutes Maximum

Location_____ *I did this*___(___Minutes) No___

4. Exercises During the Day—*Awakening to your life*

Location_____ *I did this*___(___Minutes) No___

5. Prayer upon Retiring—*Attune to your heart, invite God into your dreams*

Location_____ *I did this*___(___Minutes) No___

6. Exercise Journal—1-2 Minutes Once Daily/Weekly/Monthly

Location_____ *I did this*___(___Minutes) No___

7. As I Lie Down to Sleep—1 Minute Total

Location_____ *I did this*___(___Minutes) No___

Desolation From the Day – <u>Write no more than two sentences</u> on what decreased *your faith, your hope, and your love for God and neighbor today.*

Consolation From the Day – <u>Write no more than two sentences</u> on what increased *your faith, your hope, and your love for God and neighbor today.*

SPIRITUAL RECORD

1. Prayer Upon Waking—*I attuned to the day ahead and invited God's help*

Location_____ *I did this*___(___Minutes) No___

2. Exercises During the Day—*Awakening to your life*

Location_____ *I did this*___(___Minutes) No___

3. *Sacred Story* **Prayer Mid-day—***Creation, Presence, Memory, Mercy,   Eternity*—15 **Minutes Maximum**

Location_____ *I did this*___(___Minutes) No___

4. Exercises During the Day—*Awakening to your life*

Location_____ *I did this*___(___Minutes) No___

5. Prayer upon Retiring—*Attune to your heart, invite God into your dreams*

Location_____ *I did this*___(___Minutes) No___

6. Exercise Journal—1-2 Minutes Once Daily/Weekly/Monthly

Location_____ *I did this*___(___Minutes) No___

7. As I Lie Down to Sleep—1 Minute Total

Location_____ *I did this*___(___Minutes) No___

Desolation From the Day – <u>Write no more than two sentences</u> on what decreased *your faith, your hope, and your love for God and neighbor today.*

Consolation From the Day – <u>Write no more than two sentences</u> on what increased *your faith, your hope, and your love for God and neighbor today.*

SPIRITUAL RECORD

1. Prayer Upon Waking—*I attuned to the day ahead and invited God's help*

Location_____ *I did this*___(___Minutes) No___

2. Exercises During the Day—*Awakening to your life*

Location_____ *I did this*___(___Minutes) No___

3. *Sacred Story* **Prayer Mid-day**—*Creation, Presence, Memory, Mercy,* *Eternity*—15 **Minutes Maximum**

Location_____ *I did this*___(___Minutes) No___

4. Exercises During the Day—*Awakening to your life*

Location_____ *I did this*___(___Minutes) No___

5. Prayer upon Retiring—*Attune to your heart, invite God into your dreams*

Location_____ *I did this*___(___Minutes) No___

6. Exercise Journal—**1-2 Minutes Once Daily/Weekly/Monthly**

Location_____ *I did this*___(___Minutes) No___

7. As I Lie Down to Sleep—**1 Minute Total**

Location_____ *I did this*___(___Minutes) No___

Desolation From the Day – <u>Write no more than two sentences</u> on what decreased *your faith, your hope, and your love for God and neighbor today.*

Consolation From the Day – <u>Write no more than two sentences</u> on what increased *your faith, your hope, and your love for God and neighbor today.*

SPIRITUAL RECORD

1. Prayer Upon Waking—*I attuned to the day ahead and invited God's help*

Location_____ *I did this*___(___Minutes) No___

2. Exercises During the Day—*Awakening to your life*

Location_____ *I did this*___(___Minutes) No___

3. *Sacred Story* **Prayer Mid-day—***Creation, Presence, Memory, Mercy,   Eternity—***15 Minutes Maximum**

Location_____ *I did this*___(___Minutes) No___

4. Exercises During the Day—*Awakening to your life*

Location_____ *I did this*___(___Minutes) No___

5. Prayer upon Retiring—*Attune to your heart, invite God into your dreams*

Location_____ *I did this*___(___Minutes) No___

6. Exercise Journal—1-2 Minutes Once Daily/Weekly/Monthly

Location_____ *I did this*___(___Minutes) No___

7. As I Lie Down to Sleep—1 Minute Total

Location_____ *I did this*___(___Minutes) No___

Write the Week's Most Significant Desolation & Consolation

Desolation From the Day – <u>Write no more than two sentences</u> **on what decreased** *your faith, your hope, and your love for God and neighbor today.*

Consolation From the Day – <u>Write no more than two sentences</u> **on what increased** *your faith, your hope, and your love for God and neighbor today.*

 Week 35

SPIRITUAL RECORD

1. Prayer Upon Waking—*I attuned to the day ahead and invited God's help*

Location_____ *I did this*___(___Minutes) No___

2. Exercises During the Day—*Awakening to your life*

Location_____ *I did this*___(___Minutes) No___

3. *Sacred Story* **Prayer Mid-day**—*Creation, Presence, Memory, Mercy, Eternity*—**15 Minutes Maximum**

Location_____ *I did this*___(___Minutes) No___

4. Exercises During the Day—*Awakening to your life*

Location_____ *I did this*___(___Minutes) No___

5. Prayer upon Retiring—*Attune to your heart, invite God into your dreams*

Location_____ *I did this*___(___Minutes) No___

6. Exercise Journal—**1-2 Minutes Once Daily/Weekly/Monthly**

Location_____ *I did this*___(___Minutes) No___

7. As I Lie Down to Sleep—**1 Minute Total**

Location_____ *I did this*___(___Minutes) No___

Desolation From the Day – <u>Write no more than two sentences</u> on what decreased *your faith, your hope, and your love for God and neighbor today.*

Consolation From the Day – <u>Write no more than two sentences</u> on what increased *your faith, your hope, and your love for God and neighbor today.*

SPIRITUAL RECORD

1. Prayer Upon Waking—*I attuned to the day ahead and invited God's help*

Location_____ *I did this*___(___Minutes) No___

2. Exercises During the Day—*Awakening to your life*

Location_____ *I did this*___(___Minutes) No___

3. *Sacred Story* **Prayer Mid-day—***Creation, Presence, Memory, Mercy,   Eternity—***15 Minutes Maximum**

Location_____ *I did this*___(___Minutes) No___

4. Exercises During the Day—*Awakening to your life*

Location_____ *I did this*___(___Minutes) No___

5. Prayer upon Retiring—*Attune to your heart, invite God into your dreams*

Location_____ *I did this*___(___Minutes) No___

6. Exercise Journal—1-2 Minutes Once Daily/Weekly/Monthly

Location_____ *I did this*___(___Minutes) No___

7. As I Lie Down to Sleep—1 Minute Total

Location_____ *I did this*___(___Minutes) No___

Desolation From the Day – <u>Write no more than two sentences</u> on what decreased *your faith, your hope, and your love for God and neighbor today.*

Consolation From the Day – <u>Write no more than two sentences</u> on what increased *your faith, your hope, and your love for God and neighbor today.*

SPIRITUAL RECORD

1. Prayer Upon Waking—*I attuned to the day ahead and invited God's help*

Location_____ *I did this*___(___Minutes) No___

2. Exercises During the Day—*Awakening to your life*

Location_____ *I did this*___(___Minutes) No___

3. *Sacred Story* Prayer Mid-day—*Creation, Presence, Memory, Mercy,* Eternity—15 Minutes Maximum

Location_____ *I did this*___(___Minutes) No___

4. Exercises During the Day—*Awakening to your life*

Location_____ *I did this*___(___Minutes) No___

5. Prayer upon Retiring—*Attune to your heart, invite God into your dreams*

Location_____ *I did this*___(___Minutes) No___

6. Exercise Journal—1-2 Minutes Once Daily/Weekly/Monthly

Location_____ *I did this*___(___Minutes) No___

7. As I Lie Down to Sleep—1 Minute Total

Location_____ *I did this*___(___Minutes) No___

Desolation From the Day – <u>Write no more than two sentences</u> on what decreased *your faith, your hope, and your love for God and neighbor today.*

Consolation From the Day – <u>Write no more than two sentences</u> on what increased *your faith, your hope, and your love for God and neighbor today.*

SPIRITUAL RECORD

1. Prayer Upon Waking—*I attuned to the day ahead and invited God's help*

Location_____ *I did this*___(___Minutes) No___

2. Exercises During the Day—*Awakening to your life*

Location_____ *I did this*___(___Minutes) No___

3. *Sacred Story* **Prayer Mid-day—***Creation, Presence, Memory, Mercy,   Eternity*—15 **Minutes Maximum**

Location_____ *I did this*___(___Minutes) No___

4. Exercises During the Day—*Awakening to your life*

Location_____ *I did this*___(___Minutes) No___

5. Prayer upon Retiring—*Attune to your heart, invite God into your dreams*

Location_____ *I did this*___(___Minutes) No___

6. Exercise Journal—1-2 Minutes Once Daily/Weekly/Monthly

Location_____ *I did this*___(___Minutes) No___

7. As I Lie Down to Sleep—1 Minute Total

Location_____ *I did this*___(___Minutes) No___

Desolation From the Day – <u>Write no more than two sentences</u> on what decreased *your faith, your hope, and your love for God and neighbor today.*

Consolation From the Day – <u>Write no more than two sentences</u> on what increased *your faith, your hope, and your love for God and neighbor today.*

SPIRITUAL RECORD

1. Prayer Upon Waking—*I attuned to the day ahead and invited God's help*

Location_____   *I did this___(___Minutes) No___*

2. Exercises During the Day—*Awakening to your life*

Location_____   *I did this___(___Minutes) No___*

3. *Sacred Story* **Prayer Mid-day—***Creation, Presence, Memory, Mercy,   Eternity—***15 Minutes Maximum**

Location_____   *I did this___(___Minutes) No___*

4. Exercises During the Day—*Awakening to your life*

Location_____   *I did this___(___Minutes) No___*

5. Prayer upon Retiring—*Attune to your heart, invite God into your dreams*

Location_____   *I did this___(___Minutes) No___*

6. Exercise Journal—1-2 Minutes Once Daily/Weekly/Monthly

Location_____   *I did this___(___Minutes) No___*

7. As I Lie Down to Sleep—1 Minute Total

Location_____   *I did this___(___Minutes) No___*

Desolation From the Day – <u>Write no more than two sentences</u> on what decreased *your faith, your hope, and your love for God and neighbor today.*

Consolation From the Day – <u>Write no more than two sentences</u> on what increased *your faith, your hope, and your love for God and neighbor today.*

SPIRITUAL RECORD

1. Prayer Upon Waking—*I attuned to the day ahead and invited God's help*

Location_____ *I did this___(___Minutes) No___*

2. Exercises During the Day—*Awakening to your life*

Location_____ *I did this___(___Minutes) No___*

3. *Sacred Story* Prayer Mid-day—*Creation, Presence, Memory, Mercy,   Eternity***—15 Minutes Maximum**

Location_____ *I did this___(___Minutes) No___*

4. Exercises During the Day—*Awakening to your life*

Location_____ *I did this___(___Minutes) No___*

5. Prayer upon Retiring—*Attune to your heart, invite God into your dreams*

Location_____ *I did this___(___Minutes) No___*

6. Exercise Journal—1-2 Minutes Once Daily/Weekly/Monthly

Location_____ *I did this___(___Minutes) No___*

7. As I Lie Down to Sleep—1 Minute Total

Location_____ *I did this___(___Minutes) No___*

Desolation From the Day – <u>Write no more than two sentences</u> on what decreased *your faith, your hope, and your love for God and neighbor today.*

Consolation From the Day – <u>Write no more than two sentences</u> on what increased *your faith, your hope, and your love for God and neighbor today.*

SPIRITUAL RECORD

1. Prayer Upon Waking—*I attuned to the day ahead and invited God's help*

Location_____   *I did this*___(___Minutes) No___

2. Exercises During the Day—*Awakening to your life*

Location_____   *I did this*___(___Minutes) No___

3. *Sacred Story* **Prayer Mid-day**—*Creation, Presence, Memory, Mercy,   Eternity*—15 **Minutes Maximum**

Location_____   *I did this*___(___Minutes) No___

4. Exercises During the Day—*Awakening to your life*

Location_____   *I did this*___(___Minutes) No___

5. Prayer upon Retiring—*Attune to your heart, invite God into your dreams*

Location_____   *I did this*___(___Minutes) No___

6. Exercise Journal—**1-2 Minutes Once Daily/Weekly/Monthly**

Location_____   *I did this*___(___Minutes) No___

7. As I Lie Down to Sleep—**1 Minute Total**

Location_____   *I did this*___(___Minutes) No___

Write the Week's Most Significant Desolation & Consolation

Desolation From the Day – <u>Write no more than two sentences</u> on what decreased *your faith, your hope, and your love for God and neighbor today.*

Consolation From the Day – <u>Write no more than two sentences</u> on what increased *your faith, your hope, and your love for God and neighbor today.*

Week 36

SPIRITUAL RECORD

1. Prayer Upon Waking—*I attuned to the day ahead and invited God's help*

Location_____ *I did this*___(___Minutes) No___

2. Exercises During the Day—*Awakening to your life*

Location_____ *I did this*___(___Minutes) No___

3. *Sacred Story* **Prayer Mid-day—***Creation, Presence, Memory, Mercy,   Eternity—***15 Minutes Maximum**

Location_____ *I did this*___(___Minutes) No___

4. Exercises During the Day—*Awakening to your life*

Location_____ *I did this*___(___Minutes) No___

5. Prayer upon Retiring—*Attune to your heart, invite God into your dreams*

Location_____ *I did this*___(___Minutes) No___

6. Exercise Journal—1-2 Minutes Once Daily/Weekly/Monthly

Location_____ *I did this*___(___Minutes) No___

7. As I Lie Down to Sleep—1 Minute Total

Location_____ *I did this*___(___Minutes) No___

Desolation From the Day – Write no more than two sentences on what decreased *your faith, your hope, and your love for God and neighbor today.*

Consolation From the Day – Write no more than two sentences on what increased *your faith, your hope, and your love for God and neighbor today.*

SPIRITUAL RECORD

1. Prayer Upon Waking—*I attuned to the day ahead and invited God's help*

Location_____ *I did this*___(___Minutes) No___

2. Exercises During the Day—*Awakening to your life*

Location_____ *I did this*___(___Minutes) No___

3. *Sacred Story* **Prayer Mid-day—***Creation, Presence, Memory, Mercy,* *Eternity*—**15 Minutes Maximum**

Location_____ *I did this*___(___Minutes) No___

4. Exercises During the Day—*Awakening to your life*

Location_____ *I did this*___(___Minutes) No___

5. Prayer upon Retiring—*Attune to your heart, invite God into your dreams*

Location_____ *I did this*___(___Minutes) No___

6. Exercise Journal—1-2 Minutes Once Daily/Weekly/Monthly

Location_____ *I did this*___(___Minutes) No___

7. As I Lie Down to Sleep—1 Minute Total

Location_____ *I did this*___(___Minutes) No___

Desolation From the Day – <u>Write no more than two sentences</u> on what decreased *your faith, your hope, and your love for God and neighbor today.*

Consolation From the Day – <u>Write no more than two sentences</u> on what increased *your faith, your hope, and your love for God and neighbor today.*

SPIRITUAL RECORD

1. Prayer Upon Waking—*I attuned to the day ahead and invited God's help*

Location_____   *I did this*___(___Minutes) No___

2. Exercises During the Day—*Awakening to your life*

Location_____   *I did this*___(___Minutes) No___

3. *Sacred Story* **Prayer Mid-day—***Creation, Presence, Memory, Mercy,   Eternity*—15 **Minutes Maximum**

Location_____   *I did this*___(___Minutes) No___

4. Exercises During the Day—*Awakening to your life*

Location_____   *I did this*___(___Minutes) No___

5. Prayer upon Retiring—*Attune to your heart, invite God into your dreams*

Location_____   *I did this*___(___Minutes) No___

6. Exercise Journal—1-2 Minutes Once Daily/Weekly/Monthly

Location_____   *I did this*___(___Minutes) No___

7. As I Lie Down to Sleep—1 Minute Total

Location_____   *I did this*___(___Minutes) No___

Desolation From the Day – <u>Write no more than two sentences</u> on what decreased *your faith, your hope, and your love for God and neighbor today.*

Consolation From the Day – <u>Write no more than two sentences</u> on what increased *your faith, your hope, and your love for God and neighbor today.*

SPIRITUAL RECORD

1. Prayer Upon Waking—*I attuned to the day ahead and invited God's help*

Location_____ *I did this*___(___Minutes) No___

2. Exercises During the Day—*Awakening to your life*

Location_____ *I did this*___(___Minutes) No___

3. *Sacred Story* **Prayer Mid-day—***Creation, Presence, Memory, Mercy,* *Eternity—***15 Minutes Maximum**

Location_____ *I did this*___(___Minutes) No___

4. Exercises During the Day—*Awakening to your life*

Location_____ *I did this*___(___Minutes) No___

5. Prayer upon Retiring—*Attune to your heart, invite God into your dreams*

Location_____ *I did this*___(___Minutes) No___

6. Exercise Journal—1-2 Minutes Once Daily/Weekly/Monthly

Location_____ *I did this*___(___Minutes) No___

7. As I Lie Down to Sleep—1 Minute Total

Location_____ *I did this*___(___Minutes) No___

Desolation From the Day – <u>Write no more than two sentences</u> on what decreased *your faith, your hope, and your love for God and neighbor today.*

Consolation From the Day – <u>Write no more than two sentences</u> on what increased *your faith, your hope, and your love for God and neighbor today.*

SPIRITUAL RECORD

1. Prayer Upon Waking—*I attuned to the day ahead and invited God's help*

Location_____ *I did this*___(___Minutes) No___

2. Exercises During the Day—*Awakening to your life*

Location_____ *I did this*___(___Minutes) No___

3. *Sacred Story* Prayer Mid-day—*Creation, Presence, Memory, Mercy,   Eternity*—15 Minutes Maximum

Location_____ *I did this*___(___Minutes) No___

4. Exercises During the Day—*Awakening to your life*

Location_____ *I did this*___(___Minutes) No___

5. Prayer upon Retiring—*Attune to your heart, invite God into your dreams*

Location_____ *I did this*___(___Minutes) No___

6. Exercise Journal—1-2 Minutes Once Daily/Weekly/Monthly

Location_____ *I did this*___(___Minutes) No___

7. As I Lie Down to Sleep—1 Minute Total

Location_____ *I did this*___(___Minutes) No___

Desolation From the Day – <u>Write no more than two sentences</u> on what decreased *your faith, your hope, and your love for God and neighbor today.*

Consolation From the Day – <u>Write no more than two sentences</u> on what increased *your faith, your hope, and your love for God and neighbor today.*

SPIRITUAL RECORD

1. Prayer Upon Waking—*I attuned to the day ahead and invited God's help*

Location_____ *I did this*___(___Minutes) No___

2. Exercises During the Day—*Awakening to your life*

Location_____ *I did this*___(___Minutes) No___

3. *Sacred Story* **Prayer Mid-day—***Creation, Presence, Memory, Mercy,* *Eternity*—**15 Minutes Maximum**

Location_____ *I did this*___(___Minutes) No___

4. Exercises During the Day—*Awakening to your life*

Location_____ *I did this*___(___Minutes) No___

5. Prayer upon Retiring—*Attune to your heart, invite God into your dreams*

Location_____ *I did this*___(___Minutes) No___

6. Exercise Journal—1-2 Minutes Once Daily/Weekly/Monthly

Location_____ *I did this*___(___Minutes) No___

7. As I Lie Down to Sleep—1 Minute Total

Location_____ *I did this*___(___Minutes) No___

Desolation From the Day – <u>Write no more than two sentences</u> on what decreased *your faith, your hope, and your love for God and neighbor today.*

Consolation From the Day – <u>Write no more than two sentences</u> on what increased *your faith, your hope, and your love for God and neighbor today.*

SPIRITUAL RECORD

1. Prayer Upon Waking—*I attuned to the day ahead and invited God's help*

Location_____ *I did this___(___Minutes) No___*

2. Exercises During the Day—*Awakening to your life*

Location_____ *I did this___(___Minutes) No___*

3. *Sacred Story* Prayer Mid-day—*Creation, Presence, Memory, Mercy, Eternity*—15 Minutes Maximum

Location_____ *I did this___(___Minutes) No___*

4. Exercises During the Day—*Awakening to your life*

Location_____ *I did this___(___Minutes) No___*

5. Prayer upon Retiring—*Attune to your heart, invite God into your dreams*

Location_____ *I did this___(___Minutes) No___*

6. Exercise Journal—1-2 Minutes Once Daily/Weekly/Monthly

Location_____ *I did this___(___Minutes) No___*

7. As I Lie Down to Sleep—1 Minute Total

Location_____ *I did this___(___Minutes) No___*

Write the Month's Most Significant Desolation & Consolation

Desolation From the Day – <u>Write no more than two sentences</u> on what decreased *your faith, your hope, and your love for God and neighbor today.*

Consolation From the Day – <u>Write no more than two sentences</u> on what increased *your faith, your hope, and your love for God and neighbor today.*

 # Week 37

SPIRITUAL RECORD

1. Prayer Upon Waking—*I attuned to the day ahead and invited God's help*

Location_____ *I did this*___(___Minutes) No___

2. Exercises During the Day—*Awakening to your life*

Location_____ *I did this*___(___Minutes) No___

3. *Sacred Story* **Prayer Mid-day**—*Creation, Presence, Memory, Mercy, Eternity*—**15 Minutes Maximum**

Location_____ *I did this*___(___Minutes) No___

4. Exercises During the Day—*Awakening to your life*

Location_____ *I did this*___(___Minutes) No___

5. Prayer upon Retiring—*Attune to your heart, invite God into your dreams*

Location_____ *I did this*___(___Minutes) No___

6. Exercise Journal—**1-2 Minutes Once Daily/Weekly/Monthly**

Location_____ *I did this*___(___Minutes) No___

7. As I Lie Down to Sleep—**1 Minute Total**

Location_____ *I did this*___(___Minutes) No___

Desolation From the Day – <u>Write no more than two sentences</u> on what decreased *your faith, your hope, and your love for God and neighbor today.*

Consolation From the Day – <u>Write no more than two sentences</u> on what increased *your faith, your hope, and your love for God and neighbor today.*

SPIRITUAL RECORD

1. Prayer Upon Waking—*I attuned to the day ahead and invited God's help*

Location_____ *I did this*___(___Minutes) No___

2. Exercises During the Day—*Awakening to your life*

Location_____ *I did this*___(___Minutes) No___

3. *Sacred Story* Prayer Mid-day—*Creation, Presence, Memory, Mercy, Eternity*—15 Minutes Maximum

Location_____ *I did this*___(___Minutes) No___

4. Exercises During the Day—*Awakening to your life*

Location_____ *I did this*___(___Minutes) No___

5. Prayer upon Retiring—*Attune to your heart, invite God into your dreams*

Location_____ *I did this*___(___Minutes) No___

6. Exercise Journal—1-2 Minutes Once Daily/Weekly/Monthly

Location_____ *I did this*___(___Minutes) No___

7. As I Lie Down to Sleep—1 Minute Total

Location_____ *I did this*___(___Minutes) No___

Desolation From the Day – <u>Write no more than two sentences</u> on what decreased *your faith, your hope, and your love for God and neighbor today.*

Consolation From the Day – <u>Write no more than two sentences</u> on what increased *your faith, your hope, and your love for God and neighbor today.*

SPIRITUAL RECORD

1. Prayer Upon Waking—*I attuned to the day ahead and invited God's help*

Location_____ *I did this___(___Minutes) No___*

2. Exercises During the Day—*Awakening to your life*

Location_____ *I did this___(___Minutes) No___*

3. *Sacred Story* Prayer Mid-day—*Creation, Presence, Memory, Mercy, Eternity*—15 Minutes Maximum

Location_____ *I did this___(___Minutes) No___*

4. Exercises During the Day—*Awakening to your life*

Location_____ *I did this___(___Minutes) No___*

5. Prayer upon Retiring—*Attune to your heart, invite God into your dreams*

Location_____ *I did this___(___Minutes) No___*

6. Exercise Journal—1-2 Minutes Once Daily/Weekly/Monthly

Location_____ *I did this___(___Minutes) No___*

7. As I Lie Down to Sleep—1 Minute Total

Location_____ *I did this___(___Minutes) No___*

Desolation From the Day – Write no more than two sentences on *what decreased your faith, your hope, and your love for God and neighbor today.*

Consolation From the Day – Write no more than two sentences on *what increased your faith, your hope, and your love for God and neighbor today.*

SPIRITUAL RECORD

1. Prayer Upon Waking—*I attuned to the day ahead and invited God's help*

Location_____ *I did this*___(___Minutes) No___

2. Exercises During the Day—*Awakening to your life*

Location_____ *I did this*___(___Minutes) No___

3. *Sacred Story* **Prayer Mid-day**—*Creation, Presence, Memory, Mercy,* *Eternity*—15 **Minutes Maximum**

Location_____ *I did this*___(___Minutes) No___

4. Exercises During the Day—*Awakening to your life*

Location_____ *I did this*___(___Minutes) No___

5. Prayer upon Retiring—*Attune to your heart, invite God into your dreams*

Location_____ *I did this*___(___Minutes) No___

6. Exercise Journal—**1-2 Minutes Once Daily/Weekly/Monthly**

Location_____ *I did this*___(___Minutes) No___

7. As I Lie Down to Sleep—**1 Minute Total**

Location_____ *I did this*___(___Minutes) No___

Desolation From the Day – <u>Write no more than two sentences</u> on what decreased *your faith, your hope, and your love for God and neighbor today.*

Consolation From the Day – <u>Write no more than two sentences</u> on what increased *your faith, your hope, and your love for God and neighbor today.*

SPIRITUAL RECORD

1. Prayer Upon Waking—*I attuned to the day ahead and invited God's help*

Location_____ *I did this*___(___Minutes) No___

2. Exercises During the Day—*Awakening to your life*

Location_____ *I did this*___(___Minutes) No___

3. *Sacred Story* **Prayer Mid-day**—*Creation, Presence, Memory, Mercy,* *Eternity*—15 **Minutes Maximum**

Location_____ *I did this*___(___Minutes) No___

4. Exercises During the Day—*Awakening to your life*

Location_____ *I did this*___(___Minutes) No___

5. Prayer upon Retiring—*Attune to your heart, invite God into your dreams*

Location_____ *I did this*___(___Minutes) No___

6. Exercise Journal—**1-2 Minutes Once Daily/Weekly/Monthly**

Location_____ *I did this*___(___Minutes) No___

7. As I Lie Down to Sleep—**1 Minute Total**

Location_____ *I did this*___(___Minutes) No___

Desolation From the Day – <u>Write no more than two sentences</u> on what decreased *your faith, your hope, and your love for God and neighbor today.*

Consolation From the Day – <u>Write no more than two sentences</u> on what increased *your faith, your hope, and your love for God and neighbor today.*

SPIRITUAL RECORD

1. Prayer Upon Waking—*I attuned to the day ahead and invited God's help*

Location_____   *I did this*___(___Minutes) No___

2. Exercises During the Day—*Awakening to your life*

Location_____   *I did this*___(___Minutes) No___

3. *Sacred Story* **Prayer Mid-day—***Creation, Presence, Memory, Mercy,   Eternity—***15 Minutes Maximum**

Location_____   *I did this*___(___Minutes) No___

4. Exercises During the Day—*Awakening to your life*

Location_____   *I did this*___(___Minutes) No___

5. Prayer upon Retiring—*Attune to your heart, invite God into your dreams*

Location_____   *I did this*___(___Minutes) No___

6. Exercise Journal—1-2 Minutes Once Daily/Weekly/Monthly

Location_____   *I did this*___(___Minutes) No___

7. As I Lie Down to Sleep—1 Minute Total

Location_____   *I did this*___(___Minutes) No___

Desolation From the Day – <u>Write no more than two sentences</u> on what decreased *your faith, your hope, and your love for God and neighbor today.*

Consolation From the Day – <u>Write no more than two sentences</u> on what increased *your faith, your hope, and your love for God and neighbor today.*

SPIRITUAL RECORD

1. Prayer Upon Waking—*I attuned to the day ahead and invited God's help*

Location_____ *I did this___(___Minutes) No___*

2. Exercises During the Day—*Awakening to your life*

Location_____ *I did this___(___Minutes) No___*

3. *Sacred Story* **Prayer Mid-day—***Creation, Presence, Memory, Mercy,* **Eternity—15 Minutes Maximum**

Location_____ *I did this___(___Minutes) No___*

4. Exercises During the Day—*Awakening to your life*

Location_____ *I did this___(___Minutes) No___*

5. Prayer upon Retiring—*Attune to your heart, invite God into your dreams*

Location_____ *I did this___(___Minutes) No___*

6. Exercise Journal—1-2 Minutes Once Daily/Weekly/Monthly

Location_____ *I did this___(___Minutes) No___*

7. As I Lie Down to Sleep—1 Minute Total

Location_____ *I did this___(___Minutes) No___*

Write the Week's Most Significant Desolation & Consolation

Desolation From the Day – Write no more than two sentences on what decreased *your faith, your hope, and your love for God and neighbor today.*

Consolation From the Day – Write no more than two sentences on what increased *your faith, your hope, and your love for God and neighbor today.*

 # Week 38

SPIRITUAL RECORD

1. Prayer Upon Waking—*I attuned to the day ahead and invited God's help*

Location_____ *I did this____(____Minutes) No____

2. Exercises During the Day—*Awakening to your life*

Location_____ *I did this____(____Minutes) No____

3. *Sacred Story* Prayer Mid-day—*Creation, Presence, Memory, Mercy, Eternity*—15 Minutes Maximum

Location_____ *I did this____(____Minutes) No____

4. Exercises During the Day—*Awakening to your life*

Location_____ *I did this____(____Minutes) No____

5. Prayer upon Retiring—*Attune to your heart, invite God into your dreams*

Location_____ *I did this____(____Minutes) No____

6. Exercise Journal—1-2 Minutes Once Daily/Weekly/Monthly

Location_____ *I did this____(____Minutes) No____

7. As I Lie Down to Sleep—1 Minute Total

Location_____ *I did this____(____Minutes) No____

Desolation From the Day – <u>Write no more than two sentences</u> on what decreased *your faith, your hope, and your love for God and neighbor today.*

Consolation From the Day – <u>Write no more than two sentences</u> on what increased *your faith, your hope, and your love for God and neighbor today.*

SPIRITUAL RECORD

1. Prayer Upon Waking—*I attuned to the day ahead and invited God's help*

Location_____   *I did this*___(___Minutes) No___

2. Exercises During the Day—*Awakening to your life*

Location_____   *I did this*___(___Minutes) No___

3. *Sacred Story* Prayer Mid-day—*Creation, Presence, Memory, Mercy,*   *Eternity—15* **Minutes Maximum**

Location_____   *I did this*___(___Minutes) No___

4. Exercises During the Day—*Awakening to your life*

Location_____   *I did this*___(___Minutes) No___

5. Prayer upon Retiring—*Attune to your heart, invite God into your dreams*

Location_____   *I did this*___(___Minutes) No___

6. Exercise Journal—1-2 Minutes Once Daily/Weekly/Monthly

Location_____   *I did this*___(___Minutes) No___

7. As I Lie Down to Sleep—1 Minute Total

Location_____   *I did this*___(___Minutes) No___

Desolation From the Day – Write no more than two sentences **on what decreased** *your faith, your hope, and your love for God and neighbor today.*

Consolation From the Day – Write no more than two sentences **on what increased** *your faith, your hope, and your love for God and neighbor today.*

SPIRITUAL RECORD

1. Prayer Upon Waking—*I attuned to the day ahead and invited God's help*

Location_____ *I did this*___(___Minutes) No___

2. Exercises During the Day—*Awakening to your life*

Location_____ *I did this*___(___Minutes) No___

3. *Sacred Story* Prayer Mid-day—*Creation, Presence, Memory, Mercy, Eternity*—15 Minutes Maximum

Location_____ *I did this*___(___Minutes) No___

4. Exercises During the Day—*Awakening to your life*

Location_____ *I did this*___(___Minutes) No___

5. Prayer upon Retiring—*Attune to your heart, invite God into your dreams*

Location_____ *I did this*___(___Minutes) No___

6. Exercise Journal—1-2 Minutes Once Daily/Weekly/Monthly

Location_____ *I did this*___(___Minutes) No___

7. As I Lie Down to Sleep—1 Minute Total

Location_____ *I did this*___(___Minutes) No___

Desolation From the Day – <u>Write no more than two sentences</u> on what decreased *your faith, your hope, and your love for God and neighbor today.*

Consolation From the Day – <u>Write no more than two sentences</u> on what increased *your faith, your hope, and your love for God and neighbor today.*

SPIRITUAL RECORD

1. Prayer Upon Waking—*I attuned to the day ahead and invited God's help*

Location_____ *I did this*____(____Minutes) No____

2. Exercises During the Day—*Awakening to your life*

Location_____ *I did this*____(____Minutes) No____

3. *Sacred Story* **Prayer Mid-day—***Creation, Presence, Memory, Mercy,   Eternity—***15 Minutes Maximum**

Location_____ *I did this*____(____Minutes) No____

4. Exercises During the Day—*Awakening to your life*

Location_____ *I did this*____(____Minutes) No____

5. Prayer upon Retiring—*Attune to your heart, invite God into your dreams*

Location_____ *I did this*____(____Minutes) No____

6. Exercise Journal—1-2 Minutes Once Daily/Weekly/Monthly

Location_____ *I did this*____(____Minutes) No____

7. As I Lie Down to Sleep—1 Minute Total

Location_____ *I did this*____(____Minutes) No____

Desolation From the Day – <u>Write no more than two sentences</u> on what decreased *your faith, your hope, and your love for God and neighbor today.*

Consolation From the Day – <u>Write no more than two sentences</u> on what increased *your faith, your hope, and your love for God and neighbor today.*

SPIRITUAL RECORD

1. Prayer Upon Waking—*I attuned to the day ahead and invited God's help*

Location_____ *I did this*___(___Minutes) No___

2. Exercises During the Day—*Awakening to your life*

Location_____ *I did this*___(___Minutes) No___

3. *Sacred Story* Prayer Mid-day—*Creation, Presence, Memory, Mercy,* *Eternity*—**15 Minutes Maximum**

Location_____ *I did this*___(___Minutes) No___

4. Exercises During the Day—*Awakening to your life*

Location_____ *I did this*___(___Minutes) No___

5. Prayer upon Retiring—*Attune to your heart, invite God into your dreams*

Location_____ *I did this*___(___Minutes) No___

6. Exercise Journal—1-2 Minutes Once Daily/Weekly/Monthly

Location_____ *I did this*___(___Minutes) No___

7. As I Lie Down to Sleep—1 Minute Total

Location_____ *I did this*___(___Minutes) No___

Desolation From the Day – Write no more than two sentences on what decreased *your faith, your hope, and your love for God and neighbor today.*

Consolation From the Day – Write no more than two sentences on what increased *your faith, your hope, and your love for God and neighbor today.*

SPIRITUAL RECORD

1. Prayer Upon Waking—*I attuned to the day ahead and invited God's help*

Location_____ *I did this*___(___Minutes) No___

2. Exercises During the Day—*Awakening to your life*

Location_____ *I did this*___(___Minutes) No___

3. *Sacred Story* **Prayer Mid-day**—*Creation, Presence, Memory, Mercy,*   *Eternity*—15 **Minutes Maximum**

Location_____ *I did this*___(___Minutes) No___

4. Exercises During the Day—*Awakening to your life*

Location_____ *I did this*___(___Minutes) No___

5. Prayer upon Retiring—*Attune to your heart, invite God into your dreams*

Location_____ *I did this*___(___Minutes) No___

6. Exercise Journal—**1-2 Minutes Once Daily/Weekly/Monthly**

Location_____ *I did this*___(___Minutes) No___

7. As I Lie Down to Sleep—**1 Minute Total**

Location_____ *I did this*___(___Minutes) No___

Desolation From the Day – <u>Write no more than two sentences</u> on what decreased *your faith, your hope, and your love for God and neighbor today.*

Consolation From the Day – <u>Write no more than two sentences</u> on what increased *your faith, your hope, and your love for God and neighbor today.*

SPIRITUAL RECORD

1. Prayer Upon Waking—*I attuned to the day ahead and invited God's help*

Location_____ *I did this___(___Minutes)* No___

2. Exercises During the Day—*Awakening to your life*

Location_____ *I did this___(___Minutes)* No___

3. *Sacred Story* Prayer Mid-day—*Creation, Presence, Memory, Mercy,   Eternity*—15 Minutes Maximum

Location_____ *I did this___(___Minutes)* No___

4. Exercises During the Day—*Awakening to your life*

Location_____ *I did this___(___Minutes)* No___

5. Prayer upon Retiring—*Attune to your heart, invite God into your dreams*

Location_____ *I did this___(___Minutes)* No___

6. Exercise Journal—1-2 Minutes Once Daily/Weekly/Monthly

Location_____ *I did this___(___Minutes)* No___

7. As I Lie Down to Sleep—1 Minute Total

Location_____ *I did this___(___Minutes)* No___

Desolation From the Day – <u>Write no more than two sentences</u> on what decreased *your faith, your hope, and your love for God and neighbor today.*

Consolation From the Day – <u>Write no more than two sentences</u> on what increased *your faith, your hope, and your love for God and neighbor today.*

SPIRITUAL RECORD

1. Prayer Upon Waking—*I attuned to the day ahead and invited God's help*

Location_____ *I did this___(___Minutes)* No____

2. Exercises During the Day—*Awakening to your life*

Location_____ *I did this___(___Minutes)* No____

3. *Sacred Story* Prayer Mid-day—*Creation, Presence, Memory, Mercy,* Eternity—15 **Minutes Maximum**

Location_____ *I did this___(___Minutes)* No____

4. Exercises During the Day—*Awakening to your life*

Location_____ *I did this___(___Minutes)* No____

5. Prayer upon Retiring—*Attune to your heart, invite God into your dreams*

Location_____ *I did this___(___Minutes)* No____

6. Exercise Journal—1-2 Minutes Once Daily/Weekly/Monthly

Location_____ *I did this___(___Minutes)* No____

7. As I Lie Down to Sleep—1 Minute Total

Location_____ *I did this___(___Minutes)* No____

Write the Week's Most Significant Desolation & Consolation

Desolation From the Day – <u>Write no more than two sentences</u> on what decreased *your faith, your hope, and your love for God and neighbor today.*

Consolation From the Day – <u>Write no more than two sentences</u> on what increased *your faith, your hope, and your love for God and neighbor today.*

 # Week 39

SPIRITUAL RECORD

1. Prayer Upon Waking—*I attuned to the day ahead and invited God's help*

Location_____ *I did this*___(___Minutes) No___

2. Exercises During the Day—*Awakening to your life*

Location_____ *I did this*___(___Minutes) No___

3. *Sacred Story* **Prayer Mid-day**—*Creation, Presence, Memory, Mercy, Eternity*—15 **Minutes Maximum**

Location_____ *I did this*___(___Minutes) No___

4. Exercises During the Day—*Awakening to your life*

Location_____ *I did this*___(___Minutes) No___

5. Prayer upon Retiring—*Attune to your heart, invite God into your dreams*

Location_____ *I did this*___(___Minutes) No___

6. Exercise Journal—**1-2 Minutes Once Daily/Weekly/Monthly**

Location_____ *I did this*___(___Minutes) No___

7. As I Lie Down to Sleep—**1 Minute Total**

Location_____ *I did this*___(___Minutes) No___

Desolation From the Day – <u>Write no more than two sentences</u> on what decreased *your faith, your hope, and your love for God and neighbor today.*

Consolation From the Day – <u>Write no more than two sentences</u> on what increased *your faith, your hope, and your love for God and neighbor today.*

SPIRITUAL RECORD

1. Prayer Upon Waking—*I attuned to the day ahead and invited God's help*

Location_____ *I did this____(____Minutes) No____*

2. Exercises During the Day—*Awakening to your life*

Location_____ *I did this____(____Minutes) No____*

3. *Sacred Story* Prayer Mid-day—*Creation, Presence, Memory, Mercy,   Eternity—15* **Minutes Maximum**

Location_____ *I did this____(____Minutes) No____*

4. Exercises During the Day—*Awakening to your life*

Location_____ *I did this____(____Minutes) No____*

5. Prayer upon Retiring—*Attune to your heart, invite God into your dreams*

Location_____ *I did this____(____Minutes) No____*

6. Exercise Journal—1-2 Minutes Once Daily/Weekly/Monthly

Location_____ *I did this____(____Minutes) No____*

7. As I Lie Down to Sleep—1 Minute Total

Location_____ *I did this____(____Minutes) No____*

Desolation From the Day – <u>Write no more than two sentences</u> on what decreased *your faith, your hope, and your love for God and neighbor today.*

Consolation From the Day – <u>Write no more than two sentences</u> on what increased *your faith, your hope, and your love for God and neighbor today.*

SPIRITUAL RECORD

1. Prayer Upon Waking—*I attuned to the day ahead and invited God's help*

Location_____ *I did this*___(___Minutes) No___

2. Exercises During the Day—*Awakening to your life*

Location_____ *I did this*___(___Minutes) No___

3. *Sacred Story* Prayer Mid-day—*Creation, Presence, Memory, Mercy,   Eternity*—**15 Minutes Maximum**

Location_____ *I did this*___(___Minutes) No___

4. Exercises During the Day—*Awakening to your life*

Location_____ *I did this*___(___Minutes) No___

5. Prayer upon Retiring—*Attune to your heart, invite God into your dreams*

Location_____ *I did this*___(___Minutes) No___

6. Exercise Journal—**1-2 Minutes Once Daily/Weekly/Monthly**

Location_____ *I did this*___(___Minutes) No___

7. As I Lie Down to Sleep—**1 Minute Total**

Location_____ *I did this*___(___Minutes) No___

Desolation From the Day – <u>Write no more than two sentences</u> on what decreased *your faith, your hope, and your love for God and neighbor today.*

Consolation From the Day – <u>Write no more than two sentences</u> on what increased *your faith, your hope, and your love for God and neighbor today.*

SPIRITUAL RECORD

1. Prayer Upon Waking—*I attuned to the day ahead and invited God's help*

Location_____ *I did this*___(___Minutes) No___

2. Exercises During the Day—*Awakening to your life*

Location_____ *I did this*___(___Minutes) No___

3. *Sacred Story* Prayer Mid-day—*Creation, Presence, Memory, Mercy,* Eternity**—15 Minutes Maximum**

Location_____ *I did this*___(___Minutes) No___

4. Exercises During the Day—*Awakening to your life*

Location_____ *I did this*___(___Minutes) No___

5. Prayer upon Retiring—*Attune to your heart, invite God into your dreams*

Location_____ *I did this*___(___Minutes) No___

6. Exercise Journal—1-2 Minutes Once Daily/Weekly/Monthly

Location_____ *I did this*___(___Minutes) No___

7. As I Lie Down to Sleep—1 Minute Total

Location_____ *I did this*___(___Minutes) No___

Desolation From the Day – <u>Write no more than two sentences</u> on what decreased *your faith, your hope, and your love for God and neighbor today.*

Consolation From the Day – <u>Write no more than two sentences</u> on what increased *your faith, your hope, and your love for God and neighbor today.*

SPIRITUAL RECORD

1. Prayer Upon Waking—*I attuned to the day ahead and invited God's help*

Location_____   *I did this*___(___Minutes) No___

2. Exercises During the Day—*Awakening to your life*

Location_____   *I did this*___(___Minutes) No___

3. *Sacred Story* Prayer Mid-day—*Creation, Presence, Memory, Mercy,   Eternity*—15 Minutes Maximum

Location_____   *I did this*___(___Minutes) No___

4. Exercises During the Day—*Awakening to your life*

Location_____   *I did this*___(___Minutes) No___

5. Prayer upon Retiring—*Attune to your heart, invite God into your dreams*

Location_____   *I did this*___(___Minutes) No___

6. Exercise Journal—1-2 Minutes Once Daily/Weekly/Monthly

Location_____   *I did this*___(___Minutes) No___

7. As I Lie Down to Sleep—1 Minute Total

Location_____   *I did this*___(___Minutes) No___

Desolation From the Day – <u>Write no more than two sentences</u> on what decreased *your faith, your hope, and your love for God and neighbor today.*

Consolation From the Day – <u>Write no more than two sentences</u> on what increased *your faith, your hope, and your love for God and neighbor today.*

SPIRITUAL RECORD

1. Prayer Upon Waking—*I attuned to the day ahead and invited God's help*

Location_____ *I did this*___(___Minutes) No___

2. Exercises During the Day—*Awakening to your life*

Location_____ *I did this*___(___Minutes) No___

3. *Sacred Story* Prayer Mid-day—*Creation, Presence, Memory, Mercy,   Eternity—*15 **Minutes Maximum**

Location_____ *I did this*___(___Minutes) No___

4. Exercises During the Day—*Awakening to your life*

Location_____ *I did this*___(___Minutes) No___

5. Prayer upon Retiring—*Attune to your heart, invite God into your dreams*

Location_____ *I did this*___(___Minutes) No___

6. Exercise Journal—1-2 Minutes Once Daily/Weekly/Monthly

Location_____ *I did this*___(___Minutes) No___

7. As I Lie Down to Sleep—1 Minute Total

Location_____ *I did this*___(___Minutes) No___

Desolation From the Day – <u>Write no more than two sentences</u> on what decreased *your faith, your hope, and your love for God and neighbor today.*

Consolation From the Day – <u>Write no more than two sentences</u> on what increased *your faith, your hope, and your love for God and neighbor today.*

SPIRITUAL RECORD

1. Prayer Upon Waking—*I attuned to the day ahead and invited God's help*

Location_____ *I did this*____(____Minutes) No____

2. Exercises During the Day—*Awakening to your life*

Location_____ *I did this*____(____Minutes) No____

3. *Sacred Story* Prayer Mid-day—*Creation, Presence, Memory, Mercy,   Eternity*—15 Minutes Maximum

Location_____ *I did this*____(____Minutes) No____

4. Exercises During the Day—*Awakening to your life*

Location_____ *I did this*____(____Minutes) No____

5. Prayer upon Retiring—*Attune to your heart, invite God into your dreams*

Location_____ *I did this*____(____Minutes) No____

6. Exercise Journal—1-2 Minutes Once Daily/Weekly/Monthly

Location_____ *I did this*____(____Minutes) No____

7. As I Lie Down to Sleep—1 Minute Total

Location_____ *I did this*____(____Minutes) No____

Desolation From the Day – <u>Write no more than two sentences</u> on what decreased *your faith, your hope, and your love for God and neighbor today.*

Consolation From the Day – <u>Write no more than two sentences</u> on what increased *your faith, your hope, and your love for God and neighbor today.*

SPIRITUAL RECORD

1. Prayer Upon Waking—*I attuned to the day ahead and invited God's help*

Location_____ *I did this*___(___Minutes) No____

2. Exercises During the Day—*Awakening to your life*

Location_____ *I did this*___(___Minutes) No____

3. *Sacred Story* **Prayer Mid-day—***Creation, Presence, Memory, Mercy,* *Eternity***—15 Minutes Maximum**

Location_____ *I did this*___(___Minutes) No____

4. Exercises During the Day—*Awakening to your life*

Location_____ *I did this*___(___Minutes) No____

5. Prayer upon Retiring—*Attune to your heart, invite God into your dreams*

Location_____ *I did this*___(___Minutes) No____

6. Exercise Journal—1-2 Minutes Once Daily/Weekly/Monthly

Location_____ *I did this*___(___Minutes) No____

7. As I Lie Down to Sleep—1 Minute Total

Location_____ *I did this*___(___Minutes) No____

Write the Week's Most Significant Desolation & Consolation

Desolation From the Day – <u>Write no more than two sentences</u> on what decreased *your faith, your hope, and your love for God and neighbor today.*

Consolation From the Day – <u>Write no more than two sentences</u> on what increased *your faith, your hope, and your love for God and neighbor today.*

 # Week 40

SPIRITUAL RECORD

1. Prayer Upon Waking—*I attuned to the day ahead and invited God's help*

Location_____ *I did this*___(___Minutes) No___

2. Exercises During the Day—*Awakening to your life*

Location_____ *I did this*___(___Minutes) No___

3. *Sacred Story* Prayer Mid-day—*Creation, Presence, Memory, Mercy,   Eternity*—15 Minutes Maximum

Location_____ *I did this*___(___Minutes) No___

4. Exercises During the Day—*Awakening to your life*

Location_____ *I did this*___(___Minutes) No___

5. Prayer upon Retiring—*Attune to your heart, invite God into your dreams*

Location_____ *I did this*___(___Minutes) No___

6. Exercise Journal—1-2 Minutes Once Daily/Weekly/Monthly

Location_____ *I did this*___(___Minutes) No___

7. As I Lie Down to Sleep—1 Minute Total

Location_____ *I did this*___(___Minutes) No___

Desolation From the Day – <u>Write no more than two sentences</u> on what decreased *your faith, your hope, and your love for God and neighbor today.*

Consolation From the Day – <u>Write no more than two sentences</u> on what increased *your faith, your hope, and your love for God and neighbor today.*

SPIRITUAL RECORD

1. Prayer Upon Waking—*I attuned to the day ahead and invited God's help*

Location_____ *I did this*___(___Minutes) No___

2. Exercises During the Day—*Awakening to your life*

Location_____ *I did this*___(___Minutes) No___

3. *Sacred Story* Prayer Mid-day—*Creation, Presence, Memory, Mercy,*   *Eternity*—15 Minutes Maximum

Location_____ *I did this*___(___Minutes) No___

4. Exercises During the Day—*Awakening to your life*

Location_____ *I did this*___(___Minutes) No___

5. Prayer upon Retiring—*Attune to your heart, invite God into your dreams*

Location_____ *I did this*___(___Minutes) No___

6. Exercise Journal—1-2 Minutes Once Daily/Weekly/Monthly

Location_____ *I did this*___(___Minutes) No___

7. As I Lie Down to Sleep—1 Minute Total

Location_____ *I did this*___(___Minutes) No___

Desolation From the Day – <u>Write no more than two sentences</u> on what decreased *your faith, your hope, and your love for God and neighbor today.*

Consolation From the Day – <u>Write no more than two sentences</u> on what increased *your faith, your hope, and your love for God and neighbor today.*

SPIRITUAL RECORD

1. Prayer Upon Waking—*I attuned to the day ahead and invited God's help*

Location_____   *I did this*___(___Minutes) No___

2. Exercises During the Day—*Awakening to your life*

Location_____   *I did this*___(___Minutes) No___

3. *Sacred Story* **Prayer Mid-day—***Creation, Presence, Memory, Mercy,   Eternity—***15 Minutes Maximum**

Location_____   *I did this*___(___Minutes) No___

4. Exercises During the Day—*Awakening to your life*

Location_____   *I did this*___(___Minutes) No___

5. Prayer upon Retiring—*Attune to your heart, invite God into your dreams*

Location_____   *I did this*___(___Minutes) No___

6. Exercise Journal—1-2 Minutes Once Daily/Weekly/Monthly

Location_____   *I did this*___(___Minutes) No___

7. As I Lie Down to Sleep—1 Minute Total

Location_____   *I did this*___(___Minutes) No___

Desolation From the Day – <u>Write no more than two sentences</u> on what decreased *your faith, your hope, and your love for God and neighbor today.*

Consolation From the Day – <u>Write no more than two sentences</u> on what increased *your faith, your hope, and your love for God and neighbor today.*

SPIRITUAL RECORD

1. Prayer Upon Waking—*I attuned to the day ahead and invited God's help*

Location_____   *I did this*___(___Minutes) No___

2. Exercises During the Day—*Awakening to your life*

Location_____   *I did this*___(___Minutes) No___

3. *Sacred Story* Prayer Mid-day—*Creation, Presence, Memory, Mercy,*   *Eternity—***15 Minutes Maximum**

Location_____   *I did this*___(___Minutes) No___

4. Exercises During the Day—*Awakening to your life*

Location_____   *I did this*___(___Minutes) No___

5. Prayer upon Retiring—*Attune to your heart, invite God into your dreams*

Location_____   *I did this*___(___Minutes) No___

6. Exercise Journal—1-2 Minutes Once Daily/Weekly/Monthly

Location_____   *I did this*___(___Minutes) No___

7. As I Lie Down to Sleep—1 Minute Total

Location_____   *I did this*___(___Minutes) No___

Desolation From the Day – Write no more than two sentences **on what decreased** *your faith, your hope, and your love for God and neighbor today.*

Consolation From the Day – Write no more than two sentences **on what increased** *your faith, your hope, and your love for God and neighbor today.*

SPIRITUAL RECORD

1. Prayer Upon Waking—*I attuned to the day ahead and invited God's help*

Location_____ *I did this*___(___Minutes) No___

2. Exercises During the Day—*Awakening to your life*

Location_____ *I did this*___(___Minutes) No___

3. *Sacred Story* Prayer Mid-day—*Creation, Presence, Memory, Mercy,   Eternity*—15 Minutes Maximum

Location_____ *I did this*___(___Minutes) No___

4. Exercises During the Day—*Awakening to your life*

Location_____ *I did this*___(___Minutes) No___

5. Prayer upon Retiring—*Attune to your heart, invite God into your dreams*

Location_____ *I did this*___(___Minutes) No___

6. Exercise Journal—1-2 Minutes Once Daily/Weekly/Monthly

Location_____ *I did this*___(___Minutes) No___

7. As I Lie Down to Sleep—1 Minute Total

Location_____ *I did this*___(___Minutes) No___

Desolation From the Day – <u>Write no more than two sentences</u> on what decreased *your faith, your hope, and your love for God and neighbor today.*

Consolation From the Day – <u>Write no more than two sentences</u> on what increased *your faith, your hope, and your love for God and neighbor today.*

SPIRITUAL RECORD

1. Prayer Upon Waking—*I attuned to the day ahead and invited God's help*

Location_____ *I did this*___(___Minutes) No___

2. Exercises During the Day—*Awakening to your life*

Location_____ *I did this*___(___Minutes) No___

3. *Sacred Story* Prayer Mid-day—*Creation, Presence, Memory, Mercy,   Eternity*—15 Minutes Maximum

Location_____ *I did this*___(___Minutes) No___

4. Exercises During the Day—*Awakening to your life*

Location_____ *I did this*___(___Minutes) No___

5. Prayer upon Retiring—*Attune to your heart, invite God into your dreams*

Location_____ *I did this*___(___Minutes) No___

6. Exercise Journal—1-2 Minutes Once Daily/Weekly/Monthly

Location_____ *I did this*___(___Minutes) No___

7. As I Lie Down to Sleep—1 Minute Total

Location_____ *I did this*___(___Minutes) No___

Desolation From the Day – <u>Write no more than two sentences</u> on what decreased *your faith, your hope, and your love for God and neighbor today.*

Consolation From the Day – <u>Write no more than two sentences</u> on what increased *your faith, your hope, and your love for God and neighbor today.*

SPIRITUAL RECORD

1. Prayer Upon Waking—*I attuned to the day ahead and invited God's help*

Location_____ *I did this*___(___Minutes) No___

2. Exercises During the Day—*Awakening to your life*

Location_____ *I did this*___(___Minutes) No___

3. *Sacred Story* Prayer Mid-day—*Creation, Presence, Memory, Mercy,* *Eternity*—15 Minutes Maximum

Location_____ *I did this*___(___Minutes) No___

4. Exercises During the Day—*Awakening to your life*

Location_____ *I did this*___(___Minutes) No___

5. Prayer upon Retiring—*Attune to your heart, invite God into your dreams*

Location_____ *I did this*___(___Minutes) No___

6. Exercise Journal—1-2 Minutes Once Daily/Weekly/Monthly

Location_____ *I did this*___(___Minutes) No___

7. As I Lie Down to Sleep—1 Minute Total

Location_____ *I did this*___(___Minutes) No___

Write the Month's Most Significant Desolation & Consolation

Desolation From the Day – <u>Write no more than two sentences</u> on what decreased *your faith, your hope, and your love for God and neighbor today.*

Consolation From the Day – <u>Write no more than two sentences</u> on what increased *your faith, your hope, and your love for God and neighbor today.*

A Note to

Parish Pastors, Adult Faith Formation Directors,

RCIA Directors, Campus Ministers and

Vocation Directors

The Sacred Story Institute is working toward a full complement of pastoral resources for the Forty Weeks program. If you would like to help make this happen, please contact us at the email address on the following page. Also, please let us know what type of materials you would find helpful to make this resource more flexible for your use.

In the meantime, you will find very basic resources you need to use *Forty Weeks* for parish renewal, RCIA and prayer groups. Please access these resources at the members site for 40 Week Parish Course at sacredstory.net When you register as a member, you can access the program materials. Membership is free.

Sacred Story Press
Seattle, USA
sacredstoryrpress.com

Sacred Story Press explores dynamic new dimensions of classic Ignatian spirituality, based on St. Ignatius' Conscience Examen in the *Sacred Story* prayer method pioneered by Fr. Bill Watson, S.J. We are creating a new class of spiritual resources. Our publications are research-based, authentic to the Catholic Tradition and designed to help individuals achieve integrated, spiritual growth and holiness of life.

We Request Your Feedback

The Sacred Story Institute welcomes feedback on *Forty Weeks*. Contact us via email or letter. Give us ideas, suggestions and inspirations for how to make this a better resource for Catholics and Christians of all ages and walks of life.

For bulk orders and group discounts, contact us:
admin-team@sacredstory.net

288

Made in United States
North Haven, CT
26 May 2024

52970728R10161